AN INTRODUCTION TO LIBERATION THEOLOGY

J. David Turner

UNIVERSITY
PRESS OF
AMERICA

Lanham • New York • London

University Press of America®, Inc.
4720 Boston Way
Lanham, Maryland 20706

3 Henrietta Street
London WC2E 8LU England

Library of Congress Cataloging-in-Publication Data

Turner, J. David.
An introduction to liberation theology / by J. David Turner.
p.   cm.
Includes index.
1. Liberation theology.   I. Title.
BT83.57.T87   1993   261.8—dc20   93–15782 CIP

ISBN 0–8191–9137–X (pbk. : alk. paper)

BT
83.57
.T87
1994

 The paper used in this publication meets the minimum requirements of
American National Standard for Information Sciences—Permanence
of Paper for Printed Library Materials, ANSI Z39.48–1984.

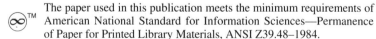

TABLE OF CONTENTS

FOREWORD

Reviewing this text by my friend Dr. J. David Turner has exposed me to some critically important issues of our time as well as revealing again the significance of solid evangelical scholarship. This work is well reasoned and balanced in it's approach to research and inspiration.

As I read the work for the first time it occurred over and over to me how much the Lord Jesus cares for the poor and oppressed. So much of his discourse, his compassion and even his anger was focused on his friends who were deprived in one way or another or taken advantage of by a system that refused to be sensitive to their needs.

I for one do not believe the Lord's compassion for the poor or oppressed is diminished. His concern has transcended the ages. Today his heart breaks for those imprisoned, hungry, homeless or abused. To follow Jesus as Lord is to exhibit the same compassion as he does.

Dr. Turner does a marvelous job of helping us understand the underlying philosophies of liberation theology. Understanding these foundational principles as well as "feeling" the hurt of the many millions of our global community who suffer is a necessary combination if our desire is to respond in any meaningful fashion. And our response is no longer suggested; it is required.

Gregory V. Hall, President
Warner Southern College

ACKNOWLEDGEMENTS

This book has been in the works for many years now. I'm grateful for all who have contributed to the ongoing dialogue about liberation theology. Hopefully every idea that is represented in this book is documented properly as no intentional exclusion occurred. I would like to thank Dr. David N. Descutner, professor of communications at Ohio University, Athens, Ohio for helping me get started on this project during my doctoral studies. Even though this book has evolved greatly over the years his help and encouragement are still warmly remembered. I would also like to thank my wife Jan who is still the greatest earthly blessing I enjoy. Lastly, I want to acknowledge Jesus Christ, the Son of God, and true Liberator for all who know and walk with Him. Because of Him I have hope for the future, a mission for today, and peace about the past.

CHAPTER ONE

An Introduction to Liberation Theology

INTRODUCTION

Liberation theology is a religious, political, and economic force operating in the world today. It "attacks" the presuppositions behind every existing social, economic, and religious institution with the revolutionary fervor of Marxist-Leninism, yet it claims to do this "with" God. Liberation theology is an international movement with the predominant activity found in Central and South America. This book is a basic introduction to this movement. As an introduction it provides many perspectives from a host of authors who defend, attack, and challenge this theology. Few strands of theology have generated so much debate and literature over the years as this one. It offers a tremendous amount of insight and lessons into the very nature of Christianity as it is written about and practiced in the 20th century.

BACKGROUND

Liberation theology is a religious movement that seeks to eliminate human oppression by implementing the ideals of the "kingdom of God" on earth. It basically started with Latin American theologians in the early 1960s, and it continues to be somewhat influential today. Liberation theology seeks to implement the principles of the "kingdom of God" on earth by liberating, or setting free, social, economic, ethnic, and religious structures that are perceived to be oppressive. It arrived at this goal of liberation by creating a "new hermeneutic" for doing theology. This new hermeneutic, or way of interpreting, in its simplest form is arrived at by looking at the Biblical texts from the perspective of the poor and oppressed.

Specifically, liberation theology is a "new" theology that uses the context of "suffering humanity" as the starting point for "doing" theology. Traditional theology starts from dogma such as the "correct" interpretation of the Bible, or church tradition, and then "implements" these dogmas in society. Liberation theology is different in that it "does" theology by starting with the poor and then writing theology from a poverty perspective. Interpretation is always checked with the actual lived experience, (and vice-versa), so that a dialectical relationship between theology (theory) and implementation (Christian action) "creates" theology. A dialectic is simply a continual two way interaction that constantly adjusts to both theory and practice. The dialectic between theology and practice is a dynamic process within liberation theology. The "anchor" of this movement is "liberation,"

which results in a theology focused on freeing oppressed peoples. This
movement tries never to violate its principles by participating in an
"oppressive" practice.

"Oppression" is a catch-all term indicating "any" practice, belief,
system, etc., that burdens, causes harm, de-humanizes, or restricts people
from obtaining the basic needs of life. In practice, specific oppressive
practices are labeled, root causes are analyzed, and then oppressive
practices are attacked. For example, poverty is considered an oppressive
situation because of the malnutrition, non-existent, or marginal, health care,
illiteracy, inadequate living conditions, lack of equal opportunity, etc., that
exists in poverty situations. Liberation theologians analyze poverty as
"oppressive," and have determined it to be a result of dominating
capitalistic economic systems, private property, and prejudice. Whenever
they reach agreement regarding what is oppressive they analyze what is
causing the problem and then proceed to "attack" the problem in order to
eliminate it.[1]

Liberation theologians attack by verbal protest; raising the
consciousness of the people so that they can spot oppression in their midst;
starting Christian communities; re-writing Christian theology; and in some
cases by taking up arms in revolutionary activity. To say the least, these
people are not popular with those in power. The religious right consider
them communists and heretics. "Free" governments in Latin America are
extremely threatened by this group, and they have murdered many of the
liberation leaders. The debate involved in this ongoing dialectic between
opposing sides is extremely full and powerful. Thus, the "action" of the
liberation theology movement is deeply felt in creating and sustaining strong
dialectical responses, especially in the Latin American context.

Thus the movement can be defined as the attempt of Catholic
theologians to eliminate human oppression wherever it is found. These
theologians are predominantly from Catholic backgrounds with participation
from a few Protestants. "Divine inspiration," signified by the words
"theologians" and "Christian," is a distinctive feature separating this
movement from other secular social revolutions that have occurred in the
Soviet Union, China, and Cuba, etc. These theologians seek to eliminate
"oppression," which can again be defined as any ideology, theology,
economic system, multinational group, person or country, that oppresses
humanity in any way. Liberation theology differs significantly from the
"Social Gospel" movement that was predominate in the United States in the
late 19th and early 20th centuries. The Social Gospel was more of a
"prophetic" movement within mainstream protestant denominations. Its
main plea was to implement the messages of Christ in society as the

following quote illustrates.

> ...if Christians would just believe the words that Jesus has spoken in the Sermon on the Mount, would believe that they are true for today, and would honestly endeavor to make those words the law of their lives, all our social questions would be solved.[2]

Unlike the Social Gospel movement liberation theology seeks "very radical" structural change. Liberation theology also is "prophetic" in public proclamation, but it takes a different approach in order to solve the problems of oppressive social structures. It has a main goal of liberating oppressive structures as a result of the "new hermeneutic" created to "do" this type of theology. This new hermeneutic, which was created to produce radical structural change, differs from the Social Gospel's approach of preaching the messages of the Biblical text within an oppressive society. In essence, liberation theology differs from the Social Gospel by its radical approach to doing theology, and its radical implementation of this theology. Yet both movements share the same desire for a more human world, one that contains "more of" the ideals of the "kingdom of God" on earth. However, they are distinctive in the way they arrive at and work for these goals.[3]

As mentioned earlier most of the participants in the liberation movement are Latin American Catholic priests and theologians. One of the major participants is Gustavo Gutierrez from Peru, who is considered the "dean" of liberation theologians. His 1971 Spanish and 1973 English publication of A Theology of Liberation is one of the key publication that has propelled this movement into its present complexity and power. Juan Luis Segundo from Uruguay, Rubem Alves and Leonardo Boff from Brazil, Enrique Dussel and Jose Miguez Bonino (a Methodist minister) from Argentina, are other leading participants in this movement.[4] All of these people have been exposed to Marxism and critical theory in their training, and all of them reflect this exposure in their writings.

Liberation theology literature has been steadily increasing in Latin America since 1968 after the Medellin Conference of Latin American Bishops in Columbia. It has been steadily increasing in the United States since 1973 after Gustavo Gutierrez published the English version of his book A Theology of Liberation. This literature strikes at the roots of the current economic, political, and religious structures operating in the global community. The advocates of liberation theology are serious enough to be martyred for their stand, and many have been.

FUNDAMENTALS OF LIBERATION THEOLOGY

Liberation theology is based on a Christian commitment to help free "oppressed" people from those who oppress them.   Notice that it is "people" that oppress others.   This emphasis on people being the source of oppression puts the responsibility for the oppressive systems squarely on the shoulders of humans and not on God.   The notion that people are the primary agents that create their social environment is a fundamental concept in liberation theology.   Thus, liberation from oppression is possible because of dealing with a human construction that can be changed rather than a "God-imposed" system to be submitted to.   Again the term "oppression" here revolves around the perception of injustice in the social, political, economic, and religious arena.   Oppression is not always a clear-cut category among L.T. writers, but concrete examples are usually given to clarify this general term such as specific geographical cases of malnutrition, unemployment, and illiteracy which give specific reference to oppression.

"At the roots of the [Latin American] theology of liberation we find a spirituality, a mysticism: the encounter of the poor with the Lord."[5]   This fundamental point is the springboard for liberation theologians, as they equate Jesus' primary ministry as a ministry and solidarity with the poor. Infant mortality, malnutrition, inadequate wages, prejudices, and a host of other realities are "the "signs" by which poverty is manifested."[6]   This "oppression" is considered inhuman, barbaric, ungodly, unjust, and is labeled "sin."   Liberation theologians demand that the church take responsible action to overcome these problems.

Poverty is specifically targeted as an enemy of all human beings. Liberation theologians take direct action to help the poor, which is referred to as liberation praxis, by working toward a social system that "shares" the wealth.   This goal is sought after by striving to eliminate "private ownership of the means of production," which is believed to be a major oppressive factor in producing class stratification.[7]   Critical reflection on the causes of poverty stimulate this political action.[8]   Taking notice of the human suffering of the poor, tracing down the roots generating this poverty, and taking action to eliminate this condition are principle liberation tasks.

Most liberation theologians agree that private ownership of the means of production is oppressive, thus they attack it.   They attack it with verbal protest and praxis, both of which are forms of direct action taken to eliminate whatever is causing the problem.[9]   One direct action has been to take sides with the poor, which requires trying to see the world from their perspective in order to reverse whatever is causing their misery.   Here is where socialism, as noted above, comes into play.   Socialism is deemed "more Christian" than capitalism, because it has a "greater affinity with the ideals of the gospel" than capitalism as it "enables Christians better to live the humanitarian and divine ideals of their faith."[10] Thus, liberation theologians desire a socialistic form of government, and they work towards creating one.

"Base Christian Communities" is another specific act taken by liberation theologians to stimulate socialistic transformation. Basically, these communities involve a "socialistic" type of Christian living where "everyone" is involved in a "conscientization" process aimed at becoming "conscious" of oppression and taking direct "scientific action" to eliminate it. In essence, it is a total "community" way of living. These groups grow all over Latin America and they are slowly becoming a "political force."[11] This "action" is probably one of the "key" elements that will make-or-break the liberation movement. If these communities become "successful" they will lend the kind of credibility that will propel this movement into the 21st century, thus improving their chances of gaining the social changes they desire.

Race and gender prejudice is another "sin" liberation theologians seek to correct. "The root problem is human sinfulness which nurtures monopolistic capitalism, aided by racism and abetted by sexism."[12] In essence, race and gender liberationists follow the themes of Martin Luther King in desiring a society, starting with the religious community, that is "free" from the "oppression" caused by attitudes that disrespect others as a result of "race" and "gender." Liberation movements in minority groups strive for a more "human" world where respect, love, and acceptance are demonstrated in the social arena. These groups primarily target the churches as the first place for this kind of liberation to start. "Prejudice" is the key sin attacked by race & gender groups, and "poverty" is the root problem Latin American theologians attack. Yet both groups fall under the umbrella of liberation movements.

Finally, commitment of critical reflection in light of Christian activity, judged by the Word of God, is "the method" used by liberation theologians to take direct action in the lived-world. This commitment is always self-monitored in order to be up-to-date with the present lived-world.[13] The "concrete experience of the faith is framed in the dialectic interplay between ongoing concrete history and incarnation of the divine message."[14] This "way-of-looking" provides a new "hermeneutical key," or way of understanding, for liberation theologians. In essence, the gospel's historical setting is displayed in a contemporary way in which the past, present, and future are locked into an ongoing dialectical process.

In conclusion, we have "poverty" as the main concern of Latin

American liberation theologians, and "prejudice" as the major concern of race and gender liberationists. Poverty is attacked by taking the side of the poor, seeking socialism as a "better" system for all, starting base-Christian-communities, and raising the consciousness of the poor in order to take corrective action to stop oppression. The method of liberation theologians, or the "new hermeneutic," is to do theology from a critical reflection on the church's action in light of the revealed Word of God. This is still a powerful movement, and the rhetorical drums have been strong and steady with their voices being heard around the world.

LANDMARKS

Liberation theology was partially born out of "the impact of Marxism on Christianity" in Latin America.[15] Marx's economic analysis was assimilated into the gospel message of salvation in a setting in which "5 percent of the population controls 80 percent of the wealth."[16] The historical background and theme of Marxism (outlined in Chapter Two) shows how attractive a Marxist ideology would be to a majority who are basically underpaid, malnourished, defenseless, and being controlled by a small minority.

Theoretically, liberation theology started with the oldest case that contains the two basic elements of, (1) someone becoming conscious of oppression, and (2) taking direct action to eliminate it due to some type of divine inspiration. One of the oldest accounts containing these basic elements is found in the Exodus account of the Bible in which God liberated the nation of Israel from Egyptian bondage, (Exodus 1-15). The story states that Israel suffered under cruel Egyptian task masters and they cried out to God for help. Moses was chosen (yet reluctant to accept the call) by God to liberate them from this bondage. Having done so with divine assistance he became one of the first liberation theologians.[17] Many scholars date the writing of the Pentateuch, the first five books of Moses, somewhere from the 15th-13th century B.C.[18]

From this perspective, every person divinely motivated to "free" their fellow human beings from oppression can be called a liberator, meaning one who is inspired by divine revelation to take concrete action towards correcting oppression. Thus, it is difficult to determine exactly who began liberation theology, but each geographical area seems to have its own "Moses," or spiritual leader who attempts to liberate the oppressed. In Latin America, Paulo Freire seems to be one of the originators of modern liberation.[19]

Freire started a literacy campaign in Brazil to help the poor gain better jobs, and thus a better standard of living. Freire spotted massive poverty, and targeted the lack of education as its root source. His literacy efforts were meant to liberate "oppressed" people from their condition. He was viewed as a threat by those in power, and was jailed for his efforts in 1964. We will see that jailing, abandonment, and assassination are common responses by political and religious structures that feel threatened by those who take concrete action to solve perceived oppressive situations. Thus, Freire became one of the first "liberators" in Latin America.

From Freire we can proceed to Catholic Theologians who pick up on the concept of giving the poor a voice, and who make a strong commitment to change oppressive conditions by taking sides with the poor. Some technical terms that are used to describe this phenomena are "conscientization" and "praxis." We have already briefly mentioned the word conscientization; it simply refers to becoming conscious of one's oppressive situation and taking direct action to solve that situation. Combining the root words "consciousness" and "science" gives the idea that when people become aware of a problem they can take intelligent, or scientific, action to solve the problem. Praxis is the Marxian notion that humans shape their history, and are therefore responsible for the way it is shaped. It also has the notion of "theory in action," of doing theory in a concrete real situation, and "changing theory" to "fit" the lived experience.[20]

The Latin American priests preparing for ministry in Europe and the United States in the 1950s and early 60s began using Marxism and "the critical school" philosophy in their theological formulation.[21] Yet it was not until Vatican II in 1965 that Latin American church leaders began to participate in major Catholic conferences.[22] Up until this time the Latin leaders were poorly represented at major Catholic conventions. Their representation at Vatican II signaled a new desire to be apart of the political and religious policies that directly affected their lives. At this conference Pope John XXIII emphasized the need for the church to focus on helping solve the problems of the world. This shift of emphasis to make the church more political had been steadily building, but not until 1968 at the Medellin Conference in Columbia did liberation themes surface with a distinct voice.[23]

"It was the Medellin Conference that gave concrete form and application to Vatican II."[24] Latin church leaders responded to Pope Paul VI's non-violent theme for social reform by proclaiming a type of "institutional violence" being carried out against them by "developed" countries. Rejecting the idea that underdeveloped nations could "catch up" with developed nations, (one solution proposed to solve the rich vs. poor problem), liberation themes began to emerge. Instead of "catching up" with developed nations underdeveloped nations were challenged to "break the cycle of dependence on advanced industrialized countries" with a new theology that could "set free" or "liberate."[25]

The Medellin Conference ended with the desire for a more "human" world. One where "justice proceeded peace," where the people of the earth shared God's bountiful harvests, where poverty was targeted as an enemy to humanity, and where oppressive regimes were publicly denounced and challenged. Gustavo Gutierrez, a Peruvian priest, had been working on various aspects of this new theology that would eventually embrace the themes expressed at Medellin. He published his complete work, A Theology of Liberation, in Spanish in 1971 and in English in 1973; this book became the cornerstone of the liberation theology movement. "It remains the best known work in liberation theology and the best overall statement of its position."[26] Many Latin American church leaders rallied behind Gutierrez's comprehensive proclamation of liberation theology. After this book was translated into English in 1973, a host of Christian theologians have seen fit to respond to liberation issues.

If Medellin was the place where liberation theology surfaced, then four years later "it completely oriented the manifesto issued by Christians for Socialism in Santiago, Chile in 1972."[27] This was basically a "Chilean" meeting of Catholic religious leaders, but Gutierrez from Peru was invited and was one of the few outsiders at the meeting. The intention of the meeting was "to reflect on the significance of Allende's socialism in the light of ... [the] Christian faith and the bishop's documents of Medellin."[28] Allende was "elected" as President of Chile in 1970, yet he was a socialist. His election set a unique stage for a possible working relationship with Marxism and Christianity. The Christians at the meeting opted to support the socialistic efforts of Allende. The end product of this meeting was the initial groundwork for the formation of an international group called "Christians for Socialism."[29] It is a bit different in focus from liberation theology due to its strong anti-capitalist stance, but most of its goals for a more human world are the same. A military coup ended the Chilean experiment in 1972, but the Christians for Socialism movement has been active with an American headquarters in Detroit, Michigan.

The next big event for liberation theology was its formal introduction in the United States in 1975 at Detroit, Michigan. This conference hosted a wide variety of Protestant and Catholic theologians, laity, and international participants. It "was not so much a conference on liberation theology as a meeting in which the many-faceted dimensions of the struggle for human liberation encountered, confronted and discovered each other."[30] This conference allowed participants openly to discuss issues in a seminar format. Gutierrez stressed his fundamental themes of Latin American liberation, Black and feminist liberation themes emerged, and opposing groups from all sides leveled their attacks at the other's basic assumptions. One of the results of this meeting was that liberation theology was no longer perceived as a "fad" that would eventually disappear. The detailed accounts of this meeting entitled: <u>Theology in the Americas</u>, was published by Orbis books in 1976 and edited by Sergin Torres & John Eagleson.

The General Conference of Latin American Bishops in Puebla, Mexico, in the winter of 1979 marks another significant event for liberation theology. This became the proving ground for the movement to see if it would last 10 years "within" the Catholic Church. Pope Paul II opened the address with a warning that the Church's mission was not political, which was a subtle rebuke to liberation theologians. The "Puebla Conference proved to be a stand-off between radical-progressive and conservative-reactionary forces" within the meeting.[31] Yet, liberation theologians did gain the overall acceptance to opt for the poor, and support and encouragement for continuing base-Christian communities. Liberation theologians also made a big decision to work "within" the Catholic Church. They could have easily allowed themselves to branch off, like the protestant tradition, and formed their own group in Latin America. The decision to work within the Church may have protected liberation theologians from secular opposition because of the political clout the church has among the majority of people. Secular groups do not want to risk losing this power by alienating members of the church. Thus, liberation theologians may have sheltered themselves by working within the church as secular groups have had a bad reputation for using high-powered rifles to demonstrate their displeasure.[32]

A less significant meeting was held in 1984 when North American and Latin American theologians met in Cuernavaca, Mexico to "grapple with knotty issues surrounding liberation theology."[33] Five dominant themes were discussed, namely: (1) the dangerous stress on biblical scholarship instead of praxis in the church; (2) "middle-class" missionary practices that ignored the social goals of liberation theology; (3) gender equality; (4) "dominance of Western epistemology" that snuffs out "other" cultural expressions; and (5) "the lack of love" demonstrated by some "liberators." This conference did not gain the kind of attention enjoyed by the earlier events in Medellin, Detroit, and Puebla, but it does signify the movements strong and steady pulse.

One of the biggest indicators of the current vitality of liberation theology was the Pope's open rebuttals of the Brazilian theologian Leonardo Boff. These rebukes always gain international attention, thus signaling the ongoing "threat" that existing structures, in this case the traditional Catholic Church, have felt regarding liberation theology. Boff was called to Rome to "discuss" the relationship of liberation theology with "the church's 'official' theologian" Joseph Cardinal Ratzinger in 1984.[34] In essence, the Vatican eliminated any possible assimilation of Marxian solutions to achieve social justice by calling them "a series of positions that are incompatible with the Christian vision of humanity."[35] Boff responded by stating that the church was still looking at the issues from "their" perspective and not from that of the "other," which is the poor. He also warned that the church could be perceived as hierarchical oppressors by the poor in Latin America if they were not careful. In 1992 Boff left the Catholic Church as a direct result of the Vatican's pressure to hinder his efforts.

The Pope's warnings continued in 1987 with his tour of Latin America. He denounced "labor system[s] that forces mothers to work long hours away from the house," but warned "workers against turning their cause into a class struggle."[36] In essence, the Pope warned against liberation theologians adopting Marxian methods of revolutionary "class struggle" as the solution to Latin America's problems. Yet, the Pope's mention of liberation theology on this tour indicates that this movement continues to draw out Vatican messages, and the international media attention that goes along with such messages.

In 1991 Pope John Paul II wrote the encyclical, "Centesimus Annus" which leans toward endorsing a "market economy" as being the most consistent with Christian view of humanity.[37] The 1989 collapse of Eastern European socialism, and the miserable failure of Marxism worldwide, perhaps gave formation to this view. Yet the Pope fully endorses the idea of liberation as an end that Christians should work towards, but the economic means to achieve liberation seems to be found in the free market and not in socialism.

In summary, the temporal landmarks of liberation theology include Vatican II 1965, Medellin 1968, Chile 1972, Detroit 1975, Puebla 1979, Mexico 1984, the consistent clashes with the Vatican, and the Pope's 1991 encyclical "Centesimus Annus." These landmarks trace the significant growth and decline in this movement. Books and articles are still being published from a variety of perspectives up to the present time. The future landmarks seem to point to a rather "hotly debated" event between the Catholic hierarchy in Rome and Latin American liberation theologians. The debate will be specifically aimed at what "means" is best to achieve true and lasting liberation. If there is going to be a split between these groups, it seems it will occur with the next few major international Catholic conferences.[38]

MAJOR TEXTS

"Texts" is a semiotic term meaning a body of literature, or a group that "speaks" and operates as a whole unit. There are many texts that speak in the liberation theology arena. Liberation literature exists in the "lived situation" in which texts in close proximity "rub off" on each other in a dynamic evolving relationship. In essence, these major texts are the participants in the liberation arena. Some of them include the proclamations of the Pope, the statements of left and right wings of the Catholic and Protestant Churches, and the current power structures of the United States and Latin American. Each of these texts has its own message. We will briefly mention the fundamental position of these main texts to demonstrate the rhetorical richness and complexity involved in liberation theology.

The Pope is a major participant in liberation theology. His basic stance is that the church should not be primarily involved in politics. Quentin L. Quade sums up the Pope's essential position by saying the church should "influence particular political and economic issues ... through believers acting as citizens."[39] John Paul II does not want the Catholic Church to represent Jesus as a "political figure, a revolutionary, [or] as the subversive from Nazareth."[40] Granting the need for social reform, the statement issued by the Vatican's Sacred Congregation for the Doctrine of the Faith clearly indicates that "the source of injustice is in the hearts of men" and not the result of Marxian social analysis.[41] Thus, the Pope grants liberation theologians the right to speak against injustice, poverty, and oppression, but he rejects the gospel being assimilated with a Marxian analysis, and any "violent class struggle" as the means to achieve social justice. In 1992 John Paul II referred to a "market economy" as best suited to achieve liberation. A distinct anti-socialist position.

The Catholic and Protestant "right," even though they are separated by major doctrinal differences, have many things in common such as: Rejection of Marxism, socialism or communism, ideas of pluralism and liberalism, and rejection of humanistic-based ideologies.[42] They favor traditional values of social and religious hierarchies in the free world. "Secular humanism" seems to be the main watch word among the Protestant right. Jerry Falwell, Pat Robertson, Tim LaHaye, and a host of others are the basic proponents among these Protestants.[43] The descriptive words for the Catholic right are "tradition" and "anti-Marxist." Tradition refers to the

Catholic Church's "official" institutions and teachings. They want these preserved, and they believe that anything threatening this arrangement such as Marxism is evil. The Catholic right is "dedicated to a theocentric-organic-hierarchical version of society in which a Catholic intellectual elite plays a significant, if not dominant, role in setting the values and cultural norms for the society."[44]

The Catholic and Protestant "left" are also divided by major doctrinal differences, yet they share things in common like the descriptive words: pluralism, liberalism, democratic, pro-democratic socialism, popular mobilization, humanism, etc. These words all seem to "embody" most of the themes of this movement. Instead of being "ideological" by wanting to legitimize the status quo, this text is "utopian" in using "religion as a basis for revolution."[45] "Revolution" refers to putting the gospel's ideals into practice in the present-lived-experience. They are radical in that they want the kingdom of God ideals put into practice "on earth," and they attempt to "change" anything that contradicts these principles. The following quote indicates many of the major concerns of the "Evangelical Left."

> The New Evangelicals charge that the social system is designed to serve the interests of the rich and the powerful, and therefore must be challenged and changed. They call for basic changes in the structures of American social institutions so that oppression might be ended and justice instituted. They want an end to male chauvinism in marriage and a change in the role prescriptions for husbands and wives. They call for a new economic order in which production will be designed to meet basic human needs, rather than to have a primary orientation to maximize profits by producing things that meet artificially created wants. They demand a government that is more committed to human rights at home and abroad than it is to the preservation of its own political and economic self-interests. They argue that the basic value system of the United States is in conflict with the value system presented in the Scriptures. The New Right views the New Evangelicals as a dangerous enemy - and all the more so because of the conservative theological stance which its members embrace.[46]

As noted, conventional economic, social, and foreign policy practices of the United States are considered "in conflict" with kingdom-of-God ideals. Indeed, the United States is another text in the liberation literature. Basically, liberation theologians consider the American capitalist economic system as one of the world's biggest "oppressors." But, the overriding perspective "within" this country is that other countries are corrupt, lazy, ignorant, and inefficient, otherwise they would "be just like us."[47] Also, the religious symbols of "In God We Trust" and "One Nation Under God" are "rich and deep."[48]   These symbols tend to entrench ethnocentric notions about being the best. "Best" in form of government, and economic structure, etc. The products of this "civil religion" have built a subtle "self-serving nationalism"[49] that "centers on the private self and its achievements."[50]   The end product of these beliefs, which are entrenched by religious symbolism, stimulates defensive self-preservation responses to anything that poses a serious challenge to its system such as liberation theology.[51]

The Latin American (L.A.) text, which refers to the regions economic & political structures, are the recipients of United States foreign policies. Due to this, and the human tendency towards selfishness, L.A. economic and political structures are basically private power bases. "In almost every nation of Latin America 5 percent of the population controls 80 percent of the wealth."[52] These "minorities" rule the majority with a strong arm type of "coercion," as the following quote suggests.

> When the dominant classes have less impact on the mechanisms of hegemony in civil society (e.g., the churches, the schools, social organizations, and parties), then they need to use more coercion; so we get military intervention to restore their tottering domination. It is a permanent state of tension, with periods of authoritarianism returning at regular intervals.[53]

Thus, the economic and political structures in Latin America are primarily "elitist" and they manifest themselves in a type of self-perseverance that physically threatens people with military coercion. In essence, these groups keep their power by force, and those who "rebel" are repressed by force. China's Chairman Mao often said that power comes from the end of a rifle, and this presupposition seems to embody L.A. power structures who oppose anything that threatens their power.

In summary, we have mentioned the major texts involved in liberation theology; the Pope, the left and right wing religious groups, and the existing power structures in North and South America. The richness and complexity of liberation literature should be evident by now. Each one of the major texts outlined above generates vast amounts of rhetoric in the liberation literature in order to gain or maintain a voice, and all of these texts are major theological and political movements within themselves.

Other significant texts include European philosophical traditions such as Marxism and critical theory, the Bible, and the poor in Latin America. The Bible will be mentioned thoroughly in later chapters thus it will not be covered here except to say it is used by all the religious texts in their quest to gain "naturalness" in interpretation and to engender public support. The poor people in essence have little voice except their poverty which is a non-verbal sign speaking for them. Liberation theologians speak verbally for the poor to gain better economic and social structures for them to live under. Marxism and the other European philosophical movements will be mentioned in the following section.

EUROPEAN PHILOSOPHICAL MOVEMENTS

Liberation theology resulted from a "hermeneutic switch" in doing theology. Liberation theologians write "theology" from the perspective of the "poor" instead of the usual approach of allowing the Bible and Catholic Church traditions to govern interpretation and practice. This hermeneutical switch resulted from the training Latin American theologians gained in European and American universities where they were exposed to various branches of hermeneutics, Marxism, critical theory, etc. For example, Gustavo Gutierrez studied philosophy and psychology at the University of Louvain from 1951-55, and theology at Lyon, France from 1955-59. Leonardo Boff studied at Ludwig-Maximilian Universitat in Munich, Germany, and also at Wurzburg, Louvain, and at Oxford. His doctoral dissertation was on the sacrament of the church in the context of world events.[54] Gutierrez and Boff are two of the most important figures in the liberation movement. These European philosophical "exposures" for Latin American theologians have resulted in a "new hermeneutic" for doing theology.

The writings of Marx and Engels leveled damming criticism of social, economic, and religious systems that were upheld without regard for humanity. Marx wrote: "Our whole task can consist only in putting religious and political questions into self-conscious human form."[55] In essence, Marx ruthlessly questioned everything that operated within the social arena of life on earth. This activity alone would be sufficient for the "radical" hermeneutic Latin American liberation theologians have arrived at, but the critical and reflective thinking of the Frankfurt School thoroughly grounded them in the critical tradition.

Jurgen Habermas, one of the influential leaders of critical theory, attempted "to provide a foundation for understanding the scientific character of Marxist critical theory and its relation to revolutionary political strategy."[56] A new understanding was needed because of a perceived problem between Marxist theory and its actual implementation.

> It was the failure of Marxist practice to coincide with the expectations derived from Marxist theory which led the critical theorists of the Frankfurt school and later Habermas to regard as urgent the need to reformulate the relationship between theory and practice.[57]

This "relationship between theory and practice" is a foundational notion in liberation theology. The relationship between the church's theory and its practice are called into question just as the Frankfurt School challenged Marxist theory and its practice. The publications of the "Frankfurt school" from 1923-1950 influenced Latin American theologians to "do" theology from a critical perspective.[58]

In essence, the Frankfurt school, and the Institute of Social Research within it, critiqued everything from "musicology to sinology."[59] In doing so, critical and reflective thinking on the relationship between theory and practice became a tradition. "At the very heart of Critical Theory was an aversion to closed philosophical systems."[60] Systems that operated from a dogma-first-then-practice mentality, such as the traditional Catholic Church, Nazism, etc., were targeted and labeled as being irrelevant and oppressive. People who operated from the "natural attitude," by perpetuating ideas without reflectively thinking through the presuppositions undergirding their position, were shown to be blinded by "human interests." Habermas posited "human interests" to be "deep-seated invariants which constitute the a priori structure of human knowing."[61]

Latin American theologians armed with critical theory, which critiques the relationship between theory and practice from the standpoint of a variety of human interests, have set out doing theology from this vantage point. The following statement by Gutierrez points to the hermeneutical switch of doing theology from a "critical perspective:"

> Theology as a critical reflection on Christian praxis in the light of the Word does not replace the other functions of theology, such as wisdom and rational knowledge; rather it presupposes and needs them. But this is not all. We are not concerned here with a mere juxtaposition. The critical function of theology necessarily leads to redefinition of these other two tasks, Henceforth, wisdom and rational knowledge will more explicitly have ecclesial praxis as their point of departure and their context. ... This approach will lead us to pay special attention to the life of the Church and to

commitments which Christians, impelled by the Spirit and in communion with other people, undertake in history. We will give special consideration to participation in the process of liberation, an outstanding phenomenon of our times, which takes on special meaning in the so-called Third World countries.[62]

In essence, Gutierrez wants "critical reflection" on the actions of Christians in light of the Word of God. And as we will find out, liberation theologians believe the Bible contains a type of "radicalness" that Marx and Engels demanded.

In conclusion, Latin American theologian exposure to Marxism, Critical Theory, and other European influences, has profoundly changed their way of doing theology. This "new hermeneutic" was arrived at by using a new perspective of re-contextualizing the Biblical text in light of critical theory, and it has evolved into a full blown theology that constantly questions religious activity in light of Biblical themes. Critical theory is one of the European philosophical disciplines that has greatly influenced liberation theologians. (See Chapter Three for a fuller account of European/Continental philosophy).

CONCLUSION

We have briefly outlined the major tenants of liberation theology, the major temporal landmarks of this movement, the major "texts" in this movement, and the influence European philosophies have had on the way Latin American theologians "do" theology. Basically, liberation theologians desire radical realignment of social, economic, and religious systems with "kingdom of God" ideals. They arrive at this "position" from a "new hermeneutic" in doing theology from the perspective of the "oppressed." Their strategy for radical change is by expressing verbal protest, raising social consciousness, establishing Christian communities, re-writing Christian theology, and some take up arms. Liberation theology shares with the Social Gospel the desire for a more humanized earth, but it differs in how it arrived at and acts on this ideal. Most of the liberation leaders are Catholic theologians from Latin America who were greatly influenced by European philosophical movements. Liberation literature is very extensive and we have only sampled a small amount.

In the next chapter we look at Marxism and the Marxist/Christian dialogue that has occurred over the years. This will provide an excellent background to understand how Marxism and Christianity have been assimilated into liberation theology.

CHAPTER TWO

Marxism

INTRODUCTION

Many theologians became liberation theologians as a result of their contact with Marxist ideas, thus it is vital to get a grasp of this ideology before liberation theology can truly be understood. Thus we discuss the history of Marxism, dialogue foundations, dialogues on alienation, atheism, humanization, materialism, violence, and the Biblical perspective.

HISTORY OF MARXISM

The following brief sketch of Marxism will be selective as it is impossible to give a complete rendition of Marxism here because of the many interpretations this ideology has received over the years. Also, it's difficult to give a correct rendering of Marxism as "Marx espoused a dialectical method which stressed that consciousness and ideology change as historical conditions change."[1] In other words, strict Marxism itself is to be in continual evolution with the changing environment. Thus, the following discussion will give only a skeletal portrait that approximates some of the basic concepts in Marxist thinking.

Karl Marx (1818-1883) was an economic determinist resulting from a strict materialistic metaphysic base. He felt that if the economic sphere in society could be changed the divisions in society could be eliminated, thereby eliminating divisive relationships like worker vs. owner. Marx felt that the divisions of society produced human alienation. He challenged the political state to submit itself to civil society so that the political structure would serve the well being of all members of society, and not serve only the powerful at the expense the non-influential.

Marx also challenged the assumption that everyone benefitted when all individuals pursued their own profit making. He felt that "individualism" was partially based in religion because of the stress on personal salvation from sin. Yet he went on to view an even more fundamental individualism that was rooted in an economic system that "divided" people. He said people were divided and alienated by a capitalistic economic system that was established to keep a rich-owner-class in power. People were alienated by not fully benefiting from their work efforts; by having few choices of occupation due to having to work to survive; and they were alienated from other people in a use-people-for-profit social structure. In essence, Marx felt that the mode of production in material life determined the general character of the social, political, and spiritual processes of life, which is to say that "social existence determines their [societies] consciousness."[2]

Marx wanted social, economic, and religious structures to adopt the notion of "praxis" in all their activities. Praxis is a dialectical relationship between theory and practice. In essence, it is the continual process of human action based on theory, and vice versa. For example, Marx challenged the church's teachings on passive non-resistance by stating that it was being used as a tool by those in power to keep the majority of people from taking revolutionary action to correct unjust social institutions they lived under. Marx called religion "opium" because it drugged believers into not taking action to change their exploitative situation. Thus, from Marx's perspective if the church saw that passive non-resistance was allowing oppressive social conditions to exist, then it needed to change its theory so that believers could take action to change their situation.

In conclusion, Marx was a materialist and a critical thinker who wanted to eliminate alienating social, economic, and religious structures. He believed that the "material" aspect of existence formatted human consciousness. Using the notion of "praxis" he set out to critique and change the material conditions on earth that were alienating humanity.

Dialogue Foundations

Many have lost their lives as a result of the Marxist Christian dialogue. One El Salvadorian Priest, Oscar Romero, was killed for speaking out against injustice. He spoke as a liberation theologian, as a Christian who incorporated the notion of Marxian praxis as the basis for doing Christian theology. Romero's quote below demonstrates the impact of Marxist principles assimilated into age old Biblical principles of justice and righteousness.

> There is no doubt that materialism, individualism, consumerism, and upward mobility without limits are destroying us from within as a people. Our commercial conglomerates depersonalize the exploitation of resources and persons so that the average American is not even aware of our oppression of the masses of poor people of the world. ... We are blind to the global aspects of the situation ... entrapped in the collective blindness of egoism of our consumer society.[3]

It is sad to note that Father Romero was murdered by people who came to different conclusions in the dialogue.

Communicologists always like to identify important aspects of communication strategies that allow dialogue and interaction to proceed. Remember that before the 1989 collapse of socialism in Eastern Europe the Marxist Christian dialogue was taken even more seriously than it is now. Now Marxists of all strips are at a definite disadvantage in this dialogue due to the results of failed socialistic experiments worldwide. For many years Marxists had the upper hand in pointing to the failure of capitalistic and religious systems to liberate anyone materially, but now the tide has changed. Yet dialogue basics must still be followed on all sides of any issue if growth, reflection, evaluation, and learning can take place, thus the following review of dialogue basics.

The way a person views the world greatly determines his or her perception of phenomena. For example, the Sapir/Whorph hypothesis says that the language one speaks determines what one sees. If two diametrically opposite groups hope to get along and peacefully coexist, then one place to start is with dialogue. Dialogue can start with an honest recognition that Marxism and Christianity are two radically differing world-views that are fundamentally different. This means we must recognize that both "honestly" see the world differently. So different that it is philosophically impossible for both to be plausible. Yet surprisingly, many people "can't believe" others hold different views the world. This "ethnocentric" view that everyone "should" see the world the way "I" do blinds us by keeping our "natural attitude" unchallenged. This natural attitude keeps us from recognizing "where" our world-views come from. It blinds us from our own "reasons" for our reasons, thus allowing us to be "amazed" that someone "could even think unlike me." Usually, first generation Marxists, or first generation Christians did not enjoy the "bliss of presuppositional blindness" simply because they usually had to think through the original message enough to be "convinced" by persuasion or first hand experience. Unfortunately, not everyone knows why they believe something, nor realize that others may see the world differently.

A healthy dialogue can begin when others know what they believe and why because the crucial "whys" of what is believed can be discussed in a "cooperative" format that stresses dialogue, which can help all involved to change, alter, adjust, or deepen. This is a human approach to dialogue that is relationally and philosophically rewarding. But due to the overwhelming power attachments of Marxism and Christianity the "ideal" relational dialogue is seldom achieved because of the various motivations of the people who "dialogue" in these arenas.

Motivations always have to be considered when differing groups come together for dialogue. The motivations for dialogue among Christians and

Marxists are no less important. These two world-views are very different, but peaceful coexistence is not an option in today's nuclear age even at the beginning of this post-coldwar era that Eastern Europe and the West has just entered into.

> The followers of Christ and the followers of Marx are coming to realize that there are not only certain advantages to working together toward a common future; there may not be a future unless they do![4]

Yet reality tells us that social perceptual manipulators, motivated to do only what ensures an advantage, will not benefit from these suggestions. Ideal dialogue requires honesty and sincerity. Without these qualities dialogue participants will only be engaged in a type of self-serving polemics. It is an established interpersonal principle that:

> When we genuinely self-disclose, others come to trust us and conversely, when others trust us, we tend to self-disclose more. When we provide feedback for others, they will exhibit more trust in our behavior and when we trust others, we provide them with more feedback. Those we provide and receive self-disclosure, trust, and feedback from are those that we show empathy for and who empathize with us. If any one of the four variables is neglected, our relationships with others will suffer while the development of any one of the four variables will normally cause the development of the other three variables.[5]

Unfortunately, we all know those who will "talk" as long as no one threatens to take away their power. When political, economic, military, and religious power is at stake we can expect disruption in dialogue foundations. But, think of the increase in world stability, the quality of life, and the benefits of relational escalation if upholding principles of relationships held a higher priority than getting the upper hand and taking advantage of one another. Admittedly, this is an idealistic notion that exalts "relationships" over any de-humanizing activity. Yet history tells us that this plea will be ignored by many who will seek an advantage over the other. Thus, any dialogue training excluding the domain of "negative de-humanized motivations" is naive. So when negative dialogue strategies are spotted they should be exposed for what they are in hopes that the participants will abandon their dialogue killing strategies. All groups are prone to use dialogue strategies that are harmful.

Certain Christians are motivated to dialogue with Marxists, and vice versa, for the purpose of converting the other with a "anything it takes" attitude. If a manipulative conversion happens the convert is proudly "shown off" as a prize possession, and much propaganda is generated against the other as a result. This type of motivation produces a type of polemics that impede meaningful dialogue because "vulnerability" is necessary for meaningfully open dialogue to exist, thus, we must avoid the negative "conversion" motivation. John Stott says: "Complete openness means that every time we enter into dialogue our faith is at stake ... to live dialogically is to live dangerously."[6] Christians and Marxists should have enough "faith" in their respective systems to avoid the pitfalls of listening only to convert the other! We must avoid the "dialogue of the deaf" in which no one listens; the other simply prepares an attack while pretending to listen.[7] This must be avoided if participants are to be genuinely open to one another's ideas. It seems a sign of strength when one is dialogically open, and a sign of weakness when one is closed.

Another intricate dialogue design that produces alienation between dialogue participants thus impeding open dialogue is false vulnerability. This is the "dialogue of self-accusation" where no real communication occurs between the participants.[8] This kind of communication is simply a show of pious humility that is egocentric and fake. This is an intricate strategy that some use to gain psychological advantage over the other. In the dialogue setting between Marxists and Christians this false vulnerability is a welcomed alternative to the accusations and polemics usually involved in such meetings, but it is crucial to avoid it as well. Even though false vulnerability does not generate the polemic atmosphere, it does not produce the kind of vulnerability that genuine dialogue requires. The solution is to avoid self-criticism that is false. Yet there is definitely something valuable in participants realizing problems associated with their various systems as this demonstrates openness about worldview problems. This is healthy and will give the kind of humility that is required to listen. Thus, being open to one's pitfalls is good, but to use openness to try and gain some type of advantage over the other is not appropriate because it will eventually generate distrust among the participants. Now let's end with a positive motivation for dialogue.

Until the socialistic collapse of Eastern Europe in 1989 a particular motivation for genuine dialogue was "the incredible development of science and technology, the emergence of the Third World as newly decolonized nations, and the development of socialism as a viable system."[9] Even though socialism is not in vogue as it used to be the world is becoming one big community where isolated empires are quickly becoming obsolete. Third World governments are still shopping for better systems to operate under due to the economic and political pressures to end poverty and establish responsive democracy. They are looking at everything that is offered by the world community. With a new freedom to choose whatever system they want, the ideological shopping market becomes very busy. Until recently, the U.S. and the U.S.S.R. were busy trying to mobilize satellites among these newly self-governed nations. Both superpowers want the Third World to set up systems that are compatible to their established systems so that their power and influence would continue. Now after the secession of Eastern Europe from the reigns of the Soviet Union, and the shambles of the Soviet economy, the U.S. has an advantage in this "satellite acquisition" war among Third World nations due to its wealth and stability. Thus, the global quest for better economic and political systems motivates and fertilizes the possibility of dialogue.

The idea that "rejection produces alienation" is another fundamental principle that must be remembered in order to create fruitful dialogue.[10] When Marxists and Christians come together to discuss their various points of view both need to accept the other completely. But how can a good Marxist accept Christians, and vice versa, without violating their own unique perspective? The key is acceptance. But how can acceptance function in the midst of opposing views? Acceptance can be broken down into accept-respect, and accept-believe.

> Accept-respect suggests that we can accept a person, whatever he believes or does, and show him this acceptance or potential acceptance in the form of respect....Accept-believe means that we accept by believing and taking into our lives and experiences that which we accept. Respect yields to embracing the belief as a belief.[11]

Respect is the bottom line in both categories of acceptance. Respect does not mean that one has to deny personal belief. "A full and loyal commitment to one's own faith does not stand in the way of dialogue."[12] This insight should release staunch believers on all sides to respect each other because if dialogue means that we have to reject our own personal beliefs to participate then dialogue is hopeless. Yet, respect provides a good foundation for genuine dialogue to grow.

Another dialogue suggestion will be that of a common concern. Marxists and Christians can have a common concern founded in "humanization." We Christians "by confining ourselves to the concept of humanization ... hope to find a field of common concern with Hindus, Moslems, Marxists, and Humanists."[13] There is a way to retain one's identity while sharing concerns with others who have different identities. Humanization is one concern that can allow everyone to participate fully. Every ideological and religious group has had its moments of destructiveness involving bloody purging, intolerance, etc. Ideally, history will teach us who differ to adopt common goals like humanization which can broaden dialogue foundations for groups that radically differ so that we can work together on something constructive and positive even in the midst of fundamental differences.

The last dialogue suggestion is that both participants in the dialogue prepare for the dialogue before the dialogue begins. "There must be equal preparation for the encounter on both sides."[14] In this way everyone will be able to contribute to the dialogue process in an informed way that hopefully will produce the fruit of co-existence, respect, openness, and tolerance. Preparation shows genuine concern for the other. If people attempt to learn about the other for genuine dialogue purposes, then many mechanical stumbling blocks can be avoided, and we can avoid the "dogmatic barking" generated from the lack of reflection on our views.

In conclusion, genuine dialogue requires honest and sincere participants, who are motivated truly to listen and work with others who listen. Deceitful dialogue tricks such as the motivation to convert, false-humility and self-accusation, and evangelical politicking should be avoided. Participants should take risks to be open with each other, respecting and accepting each other while retaining their own identity. Lastly, dialogue participants should prepare well before entering into dialogue.

Now lets enter into some classic Marxist Christian dialogues that have been going on for many years. Remember, liberation theology is largely the assimilatory result of the Marxism/Christian dialogue.

DIALOGUE ON ALIENATION, ATHEISM, AND HUMANIZATION

Many Marxists believe that religion is other worldly, and thus inherently alienating for not being focused on the present life. According to Marxists, this other worldliness, which results in attitudes of putting up with anything and living to go to heaven while neglecting the present lived situation, shifts people's attention away from the real problems that exist. This shift in focus towards heaven makes people "put up with" many social evils that exist. In this way religion is viewed as keeping people oppressed by not allowing them to experience full personhood in this life. In essence, religion is considered to be a binding mechanism used by a rich-owner-class to gain and keep control over people on earth, thus producing massive alienation of every human ideal as the following illustrates.

"Q: Is it inevitable that Marxism look upon religion as alienating dehumanizing?

A: Marxist socialism is humanism...the struggle for the full development of man against whatever would mutilate or impoverish him...Marxist atheism...is historically only a consequence of its humanism - when religion constitutes an alienation of man, i.e. when it deprives man of his autonomy, of his creative pride."[15]

Yet not all Marxists agree that religion is the root cause of alienation. Roger Garaudy considers "private property and private ownership of the means of production as chief source[s] of alienation."[16] He believes the three manifestations of alienation are:

1. Dispossession - Maximum effort for minimum earnings . . . disparity ... grows between the wealth produced by the worker and his own misery.

2. Depersonalization - Estranged from the product and the w o r k itself.

3. Dehumanization - private control of the creativity,   i . e . mans labor as the direct expression of his   species-life ... control the objectified creativity.

Garaudy believes that the earth must rid itself from an economic system that does these things to people. He believes the root cause of alienation is the capitalistic economic system that is in operation. His solution is to get rid of it. Thus, many Marxists hold religion and capitalism as the root causes of alienation. But, most Marxists would posit capitalism as the main problem, and religion as the propaganda tool used by those in power to keep this system in power. What is of particular interest from the Biblical tradition is to determine how religion is viewed as a propaganda tool to keep a so-called evil system in operation. One key to understanding how this idea came about is found in the semantic notion of skewing.

Skewing results when one thing acts as another. In linguistic terms skewing could result when a noun acts like a verb. But what is being skewed here is that Christianity is viewed by Marxists as a tool to keep an alienating economic system in operation. The skewing is that the Biblical text does not support capitalism, or any particular political system.

Christianity, from a classical hermeneutical interpretation, supports righteousness, justice, mercy, forgiveness, love your neighbor as yourself, among other things. The skewing is that Christians haven't always upheld these principles. Thus there is a vast distinction at times between the practice of Christians and the message of the Biblical text. Marxists might be justified in leveling their attack at many "so-called" Christian practices in regards to alienation and de-humanization, but they have no grounds on which to attack the Biblical text. The Bible supports some of Marx's condemnations of injustice, oppression, and de-humanizing practices.

The Marxist inspired governments that are left in the 1990's are also challenged to re-evaluate their atheistic position because Marxism and socialist thinking lack an element necessary to eliminate human alienation. Dean says that Marxists lack the tools necessary to solve genuine spiritual problems because "when confronted by the ultimate questions of human life -- the irreducibly spiritual dilemmas of death, guilt, and meaninglessness -- its hands are self-confessedly empty."[17] As a result of dialogue many Marxists are questioning their anti-religious position, and the countries that have renounced totalitarian communism are seeing a vast spiritual rebirth. So much so that many in the former Soviet Union want religious teaching re-introduced in the public school system. It seems that many are willing to allow religion to exist as a means of dealing with spiritual aspects that seem to be a real part of life. In short, many Marxists are allowing a religious dimension in their world-view. Donald E. MacInnis, a missionary to China, who witnessed the purging of all missionary activity in 1949 during the people's revolution and who has followed China's plight to the present wrote:

> The elimination of social and economic inequities will still leave man searching for self-understanding and ultimate meaning. Man's search for liberation is shadowed by his poignant awareness of ultimate mystery and his own weakness, finitude and mortality. Salvation for each person, and for all mankind, has been given and will be fully known only in God's work of grace and love in Jesus Christ.[18]

MacInnis' statement reflects a prophecy rooted in a critical analysis of what has happened in history. The point is that the something more is demanded than political and economic justice. Many anti-religious Marxists are beginning to heed this predicament. Some like Fidel Castro used to be convinced that human alienation will be eliminated when given time for a true Marxist system to develop and manifest itself. But according to Dean, "religion, specifically the Biblical tradition, will continue to have a role to play as long alienation is a fact of secular life."[19]

Mwolpka thinks that Marxists are trying to achieve an ideal society without the spiritual power to accomplish it.

> ... the Marxists ... dream of a society in which 'each will give according to his capacity and receive according to his needs' ... their vision and their dream could be said to aim at a transformation...from self-centered love to other-centered love ... If the Marxists fail to achieve their goal, the main reason would seem to be that they try to impose the ideal from the outside upon people without the necessary corresponding interior dispositions. If we Christians claim to possess these interior dispositions of charity by the grace of Christ, then we should be able to express them in a concrete material way in a manner that would make the Marxists wonder at our success. Would this not constitute a meeting point between us and them, or at least a point of dialogue?[20]

On the other hand many Christians are confronted with their lack of interest in their prophetic role for social justice. Dussel said that "the function of the Christian is to deinstitutionalize the institutions of sin and, like Jesus in his identification with the poor, turn history toward eschatology."[21] Unfortunately, the Church has not always lived up to this function. Maybe it is because the post-millennial view of eschatology that Dussel assumes is widely rejected by most conservative evangelicals. But many within the Christian tradition are still raising valid criticisms against social injustice apathy. Balasuriya writes:

> Why should the Marxists be alone - or almost alone - in taking [social] justice seriously enough to radically fight injustice? It is now time to rediscover the profound radicality of the Gospel, and to try to live it.[22]

The second greatest commandment given by Jesus, "love your neighbor as yourself," gives Christians a concrete basis for being concerned about social justice. But it seems that Marxists are completely naive if they think people will quit being greedy, selfish, and enslaving once "correct" social, and economic systems are established.

> ...for Marx and his followers human beings are evil exploiters of one another (they manipulate unjust economic systems of their own

creation to the detriment of their followers and for personal gain), and yet they are capable of an idyllic, classless existence once a suitable economic environment is provided.[23]

This "get a grip" rebuttal is based on a survey of every socialist system to date, and it seems Jesus' "man does not live by bread alone" statement continually proves itself to be true.

Yet, Marxists have served Christians very well in re-focusing on the concern for social justice. "Ideologies like Marxism cut across the boundaries of traditional religions, challenging their assumptions, and questioning their structures and demanding that they be more concerned with this world and human life."[24] It has only been in recent years that Christians dared to consider the writings of Marx as being helpful in a critical analysis of the Church's activities. Yet many Christians still hesitate to accept anything that has any hint of Marxism, socialism, or communism. This is partly due to the atheistic position associated with early Marxism. But there is a strange irony about this situation. How is capitalism, and the free enterprise system it creates, equated with Christianity when at first glance it tends to produce an individualistic world-view that rewards greed and selfish ambition, while until recently showed little concern for all the total welfare of the people in its system? And how is it that the "ideals" of Marxism, socialism, and communism are considered "not of God" when in fact the society that is desired by these ideologies more closely represents the ideals of the Kingdom of God, especially as described in Acts 2:43-47 which describes an almost complete voluntary communal system?

> ...had the church been true to its prophetic mission, and had it carried on the social revolution inaugurated by its founder, there would never have been any need of Marxism ... Marxism can help and perhaps has helped the Church to rediscover its prophetic mission. ... purge it of its opiate character ... to be more authentically human ... more authentically Christian.[25]

Many would say that socialistic ideals "sound" more Christian, but that the end product of "capitalism" generates a more Christian-like society.[26] Theologian and philosopher Ronald H. Nash currently argues that "pure" capitalism is both economically and morally superior to socialism because it honors fundamental human freedom and creates more genuine humane results.[27] The key in this current debate is over the "results" that have been produced by socialism and capitalism. In other words, what "means" produces the most liberated "end?" At present a dialogue is in progress over the merits of democratic capitalism vs. democratic socialism. And these issues are hotly debated.

In conclusion, Marxists are confronted by Christians with real spiritual concerns like death and the meaning of life. Marxists challenge the opiate-like characteristic of many Christian practices. The Bible supports some notions of Marxian social justice. Thus, the dialectical nature within the Marxist Christian dialogue genuinely challenges both groups.

DIALOGUE ON VIOLENCE

Christians and Marxists have mixed opinions about the use of violence to achieve the political, economic, and spiritual conditions that are desired. Dean summarizes the predominant Christian perspective:

> Marxists exaggerated utopian claims for man's secular future ... a blend of nihilism and utopianism which justifies the sacrifice of existing individuals and groups to the indefinite and uncertain prospect of some future era of human emancipation ... Marxism's pseudoscientific confidence in the historical inevitability of the world communist movement has ... functioned as an ideological prop for the cynical exercise of political terror and party dictatorship ... which has not provided genuine human emancipation ... Marxists must show that Marxism is capable of humanization now and not defer the process of genuine human emancipation.[28]

It seems that violent activity has not proven to help matters. It is very difficult for many Christians to accept the concept of killing anyone in order to establish a better society. This is partly due to their belief in the eternal nature of human beings that Christian theology posits, and also because of the direct teachings of Jesus not to murder (not even to be angry at another person enough to kill them, Matt.5:21-23). But other Christians point to God's judgment on the inhabitants of Canaan before Joshua led the Israelites into it. God told them to destroy all the people or otherwise the inhabitants would corrupt them with idolatry. Also Biblical scholars would point to the Hebrew language distinction between murder and killing. Killing was permitted if it was in defense of person, country, or by God's order, but murder was never allowed in the Old Testament. But in light of what has happened with the various revolutions of the last one hundred years, many Christians would point to the danger of killing for social revolution. Violent human purging does not seem to produce the type of society that is desired. Dean says:

> Christian eschatology might consider itself superior to any secular form of utopian ideology: it speaks of and promises more, and yet it knows and endangers us less.[29]

Thus, most Christians reject violent human purging as the way for creating social change.

Another reason for rejecting violence is that many Christians feel that the teachings of Jesus alone will produce the kind of radical revolution that is needed to end social injustice without the use of violence. "His cross and resurrection are the source and continuing inspiration of a political, more specifically a revolutionary historical, hermeneutic."[30] However, Marxists could point to the fact that Jesus' teaching have been around for almost two thousand years and the world community is still predominantly oppressive according to their standards. They could also point to the "iron rice bowl" progress of China since the 1949 people's revolution where in less than 30 years everyone had basic food, shelter, work, and basic health care. Minimal as these basics are they are still "better" off in these ways than they were before the revolution. Yet the People's Republic of China is far from being a model society for any country to follow!

And if we naively think that Mao's Chinese marxist revolution is a thing of the past we need only look at the current chaos in Peru. The "marxist Shinning Path have plunged Peru into a nightmare. Those who stand in the way of their revolution have been murdered."[31] Abimael Guzman, who was recently arrested,[32] leads this group with Mao's hideous perspective that "power comes from the end of a rifle." The Shinning Path have bought into Marx's dark ideal that the "material" if properly arranged will liberate all. Killing all who oppose is accepted and regularly practiced. Of course, this extreme brand of marxism is condemned by most academic marxists, and I don't know of one liberation theologian who supports this group publically. Yet during the Ortega Nicaragua era some liberation theologians took up arms to fight with the Sandinistas.

> In July 1979, when a bloody revolution swept away the forty-two-year-old Somocista dictatorship in Nicaragua, ... The influential Catholic bishops had issued pastoral letters denouncing the government's violations of human rights and spoke about the people's right to rebel in the face of prolonged, unbearable tyranny.[33]

Yet the question is: Could not the same liberation policies have be implemented without violent human purging? Many revolutions take some of the best humanistic ideas of the Christian faith and made them public policy.[34] Yet, it seems difficult to justify killing people in order to establish a "better" society. Killing anyone for a better future seems to be a moral and ethical oxymoron! Yet a viable effort by the Christian community to establish hope for social justice seems to have breed this desperation seed that has grown into killing among many in the Third World. It seems that when the church fails to strive for human justice on earth it becomes redundant and corrupt, and therefore no longer a representative of God's will. Thus, opening up people to the persuasive lies of murderous demons.

Whenever the church fails to understand that the gospel of hope is the Good News of freedom, people are in danger of being treated as property. Then the future is projected as a continuation of the present. But hope that is grounded in the freedom of God becomes a critique of society as "the blind receive their sight and the lame walk, lepers are cleansed and the deaf hear, and the dead are raised up, and the poor have good news preached to them.[35]

In conclusion, violent change is not acceptable to most Christians. Marxists groups who use violence may be undermining their long term efforts by killing people in order to establish a better existence in the future. The gospel message contains teachings directed toward radically solving social problems of alienation and oppression. The church must constantly strive for justice in order to represent the God of the Bible accurately. Both groups have legitimate questions about the other's activity. These questions serve both groups in demanding a re-analysis of ideologies and theologies.

DIALOGUE ON MATERIALISM

Materialism is the foundation upon which Marxism rests, and Jesus' resurrection from the dead is the foundation upon which Christianity rests. If one wants to refute either world-view then these two foundations must be shown false. The following quote reflects on the foundations of Marx's materialism:

Nature exists independently of all philosophies. It is the foundation upon which we, ourselves products of nature, are built. Outside man and nature nothing exists, and the higher beings which our religious phantasies have created are only the fantastic reflections of our individuality.

In 1841 Ludwig Feuerbach published a book that was to do much to 'fix' Marx's thought, his <u>Essence of Christianity</u> - in which he maintained "inter alia" that the substance of the right religion was a nutritious diet, chiefly beans ... Feuerbach in fact is maintaining the entirely intelligible proposition [!] that hunger determined religion, not religion hunger, that the essence of Christianity is brotherly love; and that this becomes thin on an empty stomach.[36]

In contrast, the Apostle Paul writes about Jesus' resurrection:

> For what I received I passed on to you as of first importance: that Christ died for our sins according to the scriptures, that he was buried, that he was raised on the third day according to the scriptures, and that he appeared to Peter, and then to the twelve. After that, he appeared to more than five hundred of the brothers at the same time, most of whom are still living, though some have fallen asleep. Then he appeared to James, then to all the apostles, and last of all he appeared to me also, as to one abnormally born. ...
>
> But if it is preached that Christ has been raised from the dead, how can some of you say that there is no resurrection of the dead? If there is no resurrection of the dead, then not even Christ has not been raised. And if Christ has not been raised, our preaching is useless and so is your faith. More than that, we are even found to be false witnesses about God that he raised Christ from the dead. ... And if Christ has not been raised, your faith is futile; you are still in your sins. ... If only for this life we have hope in Christ, we are to be pitied more than all men. 1 Corinthians 15.[37]

The historicity of Jesus's resurrection from the dead is overwhelming even to the casual investigator. Marxist attacks based on "red herring" logical fallacies of an "enslaving Church" used for the "reason" to dismiss the Christian faith is bankrupt and has been easily refuted over the years. And the philosophical problems materialism has in adequately explaining "non-physical" aspects such as "the mind" seriously challenge Marx's basic materialism from the Christian perspective. Marx's materialism seems to be necessary but not sufficient to speak to the "total" human dilemma, and Christians have rightly challenged it relentlessly.

...materialism is the linchpin of the entire Marxist world-view ... falsification of materialism would at the same time constitute a falsification of the system as a whole, ...[38]

Marx's critique of Christianity is severely lacking when confronted with the historical aspects of the resurrection.   Gary Habermas, an evangelical who defends the historicity of the literal resurrection of Jesus from the dead, has outlined ten historical aspects of the resurrection.   The reason for mentioning the resurrection here is simple: If Jesus actually raised from the dead, then this event undermines the strict material metaphysic associated with Marxism.   Habermas' list serves us to see what these are.

[The following] ... data reveals at least ten facts which are accepted as historical by virtually all scholars who study this subject, in spite of the various differences in other areas of their thought.   (1) Jesus died because of crucifixion.   (2) He was buried.   (3) The disciples became very discouraged, having lost all hope because of His death.   (4) Jesus' tomb was found empty soon after His burial.   (5) A few days after Jesus' death, the disciples had experiences which they believed were literal appearances of the risen Jesus.   (6) Because of these experiences, the disciples' lives were completely transformed to the point of being willing to die for their belief.

(7) The disciples' public testimony concerning the resurrection took place in Jerusalem, where Jesus was crucified and buried shortly before.   (8) The Christian church had its beginning at this time.   (9) Sunday became the primary day of worship.   (10) A few years later, Paul became a believer because of an experience which he also believed to be an appearance of the risen Jesus.[39]

Tests for the historicity of the above claims, except for the empty tomb, are nearly unanimous even among critical scholars who do not hold to the classical hermeneutical interpretation of the New Testament texts. "With the exception of the empty tomb, it is the virtually unanimous view of all theologians that these [the ten statements above] that these are the known historical facts.   Therefore, any conclusions must properly account for them."[40]   Yet when we examine Marx's reasons for dismissing "religion," including his own Jewish/Christian heritage, we find his arguments unpersuasive and problematic.

First, Marx's "religious phantasies" explanation for Christianity is severely limited in explanatory power for it does not account for the following:

1. Phantasies or "hallucinations are subjective experiences" with interior qualities that are not readily shared, thus it is difficult to imagine more than a few people sharing the same phantasy.

2. Jesus' resurrection was not expected by the disciples and they were greatly discouraged by his death, thus the notion of projecting what they wanted is lacking. Plus, there is no inherent reason why someone would fantasize about someone raising from the dead, especially if such a idea would cause severe reactions from others. Not only were there severe reactions to the apostles message, most of them lost their life as a result of continued proclamation Jesus' resurrection in the face of severe opposition. Thus, "religious phantasy" explanation does not explain why a group of unrelated people would continue to do something like this over a long period of time if their message was based on a "phantasy!"

3. The type of people who began speaking about Jesus' resurrection were from significantly different backgrounds, thus another reason they would not share in the same phantasy.

4. The written record referred to Jesus' resurrection as a historical fact in such a way that leaves no question concerning what the New Testament writers meant, thus to flippantly say these statements are "phantasies" without dealing with the historical intention of the New Testament texts is bad scholarship, and is best described as "aprioristic bias" against such ideas.

5. Phantasies and hallucinations are often drug induced, or result from some mental disorder, and it is hard to build a case against so many different types of people from a "deprivation" point of view that would explain why they would hallucinate about someone raising from the dead.

6. Paul and James, two people who reportedly saw the risen Jesus, didn't believe in Him beforehand. Plus, Paul had a vested interest in refuting the resurrection, thus a "phantasy" explanation doesn't explain how an unbeliever with a vested interest in remaining a Pharisee, a leader in the Jewish religion, would suddenly start writing and teaching that Jesus rose from the dead.[41]

The six points above are sufficient to show beyond a reasonable doubt that the "phantasy" explanation for Christianity is severely lacking in being able to explain why the early Christian leaders acted in the way that they did. Not only is the notion of phantasy bogus, but every other explanatory paradigm used to explain away the historical literal bodily resurrection of Jesus from the dead, such as Feuerbach's notion that "God is simply an abstraction,"[42] is equally lacking.

..., no proposed naturalistic theory attempting to explain the resurrection has yet properly accounted for all the accepted facts concerning this event. Naturalistic theories such as those alleging various types of fraud, a swoon, hallucinations, (along with other psychological explanations), spiritualistic phenomena, and legends have failed to disprove the resurrection.[43]

Marx's analysis is equally lacking when he dismisses Christianity as the result of the lack of "redeemed" human behavior he observed in the Christian community. He basically "skewed" how Christians were acting in his day with the original message of it's Founder, thus committing a "red herring" logical fallacy by diverting attention away from the ethical precepts of Christianity in order to focus on how Christians, who were not living out the ethical precepts, were behaving in his day. This red herring strategy allowed Marx to say that: "Religion is servility and submission to authority."[44] Admittedly, Christianity does teach servitude and submission to authority, but this is based on themes of both a "liberation" in this world and in the world to come rather than as a system of "slavery" as Marx concluded. Thus, Marx dismissed the Christian faith on the basis of how he perceived Christians behavior rather than on the foundations of the faith. He should have known that in order to eliminate the Christian faith one must wipe out the foundations upon which that faith rests upon such as Jesus' resurrection.

Lastly, Marx's materialism can be seriously challenged with philosophical problems that materialism has in being sufficient to explain such phenomena as "mental events [that] do not have properties that hold for physical events."[45] In other words if materialism states that matter and energy is all their is, then how does one explain mental activity in such a way that "thoughts" have substance in the same way that other "physical" properties do? Plus, how does materialism explain "intentions" that point "out there" in transcendent ways without granting some type of mind/body dualism. Yet if the "mind" is granted as a "non-physical substance" and if this mind is "finite" doesn't this point to the logical possibility for the existence of an "Infinite Mind?"[46] Thus, it seems that Marx's "ideas about" materialism undermine the very foundation of the materialistic metaphysic that he so desperately needs in order for his ideology to work. Yet,

Materialism so skews the overall picture of human life that it cannot avoid diminishing the importance of the ideological and spiritual dimensions of man's existence. Nothing could be more serious where human rights are concerned, for the neglect of civil liberties and the transcendent will assuredly dehumanize the citizens of any nation. It is still an empirical truth that "man does not live by bread alone."[47]

Christians also challenge atheism as being an essential component of Marxian socialism, thus demonstrating the strategy of condemning unjust Christian practice without throwing out belief in God.

> The contemporary Marxist has been asked by the theologian to reconsider whether atheism is doctrinally necessary to his social theory. If it is possible to develop a concept of God capable of supporting a humanism as materialistic in its concern for man's this-worldly existence as is Marx's ... could nontheistic humanism view itself as logical and logically compatible with such a theism?[48]

If the leaders of the early communist movements would not have made the fundamental mistake of throwing out the Christian faith they might have gained more international support. In other words Marx, Engels, Lenin, Stalin, Mao, all considered "religion" to be an abstract "idea" that lacked earth-centered praxis. Their desire for social reforms, the ones the church was ignoring, might have gained more world wide support by denouncing Christian practices without renouncing God, yet not all have done this. Yet no one doubts that the major communistic leaders were more interested in gaining power than in gaining social reforms. Their histories all speak like neon lights in this respect. Yet some liberation theologians have altruistically sought social reforms using elements of Marxism while holding onto faith in God.

Liberation theologians, like Gustavo Gutierrez, have adopted the Marxist notion of praxis as the locus of doing theology. Praxis means action based on theory, and theory based on action. Gutierrez wants Christian theology to reflect the actual lived experience, and for the present economic, social, and religious systems to implement Biblical principles in their policies.

> Gustavo Gutierrez was mainly responsible for its [liberation theology] when he began to ask himself "Is there a theology of development" or "a theology of liberation?" From the model of development, there arose a theology of developmentalism, which had as its model the center. Liberation theology arises from the discovery of the fact of dependence. Now the model is no longer

imitation of the center but, rather, the proposal of a new person based on an understanding of the structure of the world system. It is a theology that is much more radical, universal, and world-embracing, not just one new aspect but a total transformation of theological reflection.[49]

Gutierrez focuses on "doing" theology, which entails seeing theology as a human centered quest for justice and human rights for the poor. The trend among some Central/South American theologians, like Gutierrez, is that atheism is not an essential component of Marxism. It seems that the liberation of human oppression is the crucial element in Marxism. If God supports a theology of justice and righteousness "on earth" as well as spiritual salvation from sin, then a Marxist analysis can indeed be used to analyze human "praxis" on earth. This assimilation of the gospel with Marxism demonstrates that Christianity and Marxist analysis are viewed as compatible in this area by liberation theologians like Gutierrez.

In conclusion, Marxism is agreeable to some theologians, and atheism doesn't seem to be an essential aspect of Marxism. The material metaphysic is seriously challenged with the historicity of Jesus' resurrection, exposing Marx's the red herring logical fallacy, and with philosophical problems of materialism with mind/body dualism. Marxist-inspired leaders may have made a fundamental mistake of ignoring the Biblical text in their rejection of Christian practices. Liberation theologians incorporate Marxist praxis into the way they write and practice theology, thus demonstrating a significant assimilation of Marxism in Christianity.

THE BIBLICAL PERSPECTIVE

The Biblical perspective is so adamant about justice for all -- which involves being completely fair in all social, legal, and political spheres, liberating the oppressed, condemning government corruption, rebuking greed, selfishness, etc. -- that it seems strange that Marx would dismiss it. McGovern states: "justice is decisive for God. One cannot claim to know, love, or worship God except through doing justice."[50] Marxism at face value seems to be striving for some of the very things God desires, yet seeks to achieve these goals by ignoring a Biblical tradition that offers support to it.[51]

Yet there always has been a cry for justice in the United States. Proponents of the social gospel in the U.S. have always sided with a "justice-for-the-poor" position as this quote by Walter Rauschenbusch indicated:

When we learn from the gospels, for instance, that God is on the side of the poor, and that he proposes to view anything done or not done to them as having been done or not done to him, such a revelation of solidarity and humanity comes with a regenerating shock to our selfish minds.[52]

Rauschenbusch went on to indict theologians who felt "comfortable" in their sanctions of a lifestyle that was comfortable "to them" while ignoring the plight of others.

The bourgeois theologians have misrepresented our revolutionary God. God is for the kingdom of God, and his kingdom does not mean injustice and the perpetuation of innocent suffering. The best theology for modern needs is to make this point very clear.[53]

If this type of Christianity would have been predominant in the 19th century it might have given Marx a different notion about the "abstract" God he rejected. The Bible is full of proclamations, warnings, prophecies, and teachings that promises God's blessings on those who make "justice and righteousness" cornerstones of society. God, as recorded in the Bible, has always been on the side of justice. Israel, the nation God chose to teach all other nations, was divinely liberated from Egyptian bondage.

My father [Abraham] was a wandering Armenian, and he went down to Egypt and sojourned there, few in number; but there he became a great, mighty and populous nation. And the Egyptians treated us harshly and afflicted us, and imposed hard labor on us. Then we cried to the Lord, the God of our fathers, and the Lord heard our voice and saw our affliction and our toil and our oppression; and the Lord brought us out of Egypt with a mighty hand and an outstretched arm and with great terror and with signs and wonders; and He has brought us to this place, and has given us this land, a land flowing with milk and honey.[54]

Did God oppress the people He drove out by allowing the Jews to gain a land of their own at the expense of the previous inhabitants? According to the Old Testament, God drove out the inhabitants of Canaan because of their disobedience. Moses warned Israel not to mimic the rebellious acts of the other nations, e.g. sexual intercourse with animals, murder, child sacrifices, etc., unless they wanted the same punishment.

> Do not defile yourselves by any of these things; for by all
> these the nations which I am casting out before you have become
> defiled. For the land has become defiled, therefore I have visited its
> punishment upon it, so the land has spewed out its inhabitants. But
> as for you, you are to keep My statutes and My judgments, and shall
> not do any of these abominations, neither the native, nor the alien
> who sojourns among you ... so that the land may not spew you out,
> should you defile it, as it has spewed out the nation which has been
> before you.[55]

This passage clearly points to a God who holds all societies accountable for
their actions including Israel. The prior inhabitants of the Judean territory
were said to have been removed by God for their disobedience. After
many years Israel was carried away into captivity for its disobedience. But
the point is that the Bible clearly supports the claim that God is a God of
justice and righteousness. Even Jesus is said to be the one who pays the
price for rebellion in order to satisfy God's justice requirements: "that He
[God] might be just and the justifier of the one who has faith in Jesus."[56]
In other words the Bible portrays Jesus as the One who satisfies God's
justice requirements for all who accept His sacrificial death for their sins,
and who follow Him as their Lord.

Other Bible passages exemplify God's concern and priority for the
social welfare of communities.

> If there is a poor man with you, one of your brothers, in any
> of your towns in your land which the Lord your God is giving you,
> you shall not harden your heart, nor close your hand from your poor
> brother; but you shall freely open your hand to him, and shall
> generously lend him sufficient for his need in whatever he
> lacks.[57]

It seems that Marx made a fundamental mistake in ousting God from
his social theory. It may be true that he didn't see any of the Bible's ideals
practiced by the church in his generation, but this doesn't justify his
throwing out a world-view that in essence supports his basic concerns.

In conclusion, this section questions traditional Marxist theory that
ignores the Biblical teachings. The Bible supports the notion that God is
a God of justice, and those who follow God must strive to be just in order
to accurately represent God. Marx made a fundamental mistake in rejecting
the Biblical text. We leave this part of the dialogue with one evangelistic
thought about the Christian faith.

All that Christianity asks of men on this subject, is, that they would be consistent with themselves; that they would treat its evidences as they treat the evidence of other things; and that they would try and judge its actors and witnesses, as they deal with their fellow men, when testifying to human affairs and actions, in human tribunals. Let the witnesses be compared with themselves, with each other, and with surrounding facts and circumstances; and let their testimony be sifted, as if it were given in a court of justice, on the side of the adverse party, the witness being subjected to a rigorous cross-examination. The result, it is confidently believed, will be an undoubting conviction of their integrity, ability, and truth.[58]

CONCLUSION

This chapter looks at the fundamentals of Marxism and various Christian dialogues with Marxist ideas. Marxism has challenged Christianity in understanding the importance of the material factors of life. Christianity challenges Marxists to broaden their perspective by including groups that differ in method and orientation specifically in discarding the strict material metaphysic. At the present time the Marxist Christian dialogue is at a low ebb. The collapse of Eastern Europe's socialism has relegated Marxism unworkable and flawed for many. Yet liberation theologians came up with their theology as a result of trusting Marxist economic ideas to be viable in bringing about economic liberation.

A brief sketch of Marxism and some Marxist/Christian dialogues of past and present have been given as a foundation to liberation theology. Chapter three looks more specifically at how other European philosophical systems have influenced the thinking of liberation theologians.

CHAPTER THREE

European/Continental Philosophy

Introduction

The last chapter examined Marxism to see how it has influenced liberation theologians. In this chapter we will examine strands of European & Continental philosophy that will give insight into the same type of literature that prevails in much of the liberation literature. While we review these philosophic domains we will also pick out various analytic tools to use in analyzing and describing the specific liberation texts in the next chapter. In essence, we will examine types of European philosophy that liberation thinkers have utilized and then we will use this same philosophy to help us analyze their theology.[1] This will provide an excellent background to liberation theology while at the same time give understanding to the same set of tools we use in our analysis. Thus this chapter is organized into the following sections: The nature of tools, semantics, phenomenology, phenomenological analysis of Marxism and Christianity, hermeneutics, semiotics, and structuralism.

The Nature of Tools

"Tools" are "ways of looking" at texts. It is essential for us to realize that one is always using some type of descriptive tool in analyzing any text. Wo to the naive fool who doesn't understand what tools are in use, where they came from, and what their limitations are. Thus, as we continue to introduce liberation theology with a set of tools we want to know where they come from and what they can tell us.

The first question is "can we derive or make up descriptive or analytic tools?" The answer is that every descriptive tool is derived. Interpretative, descriptive, and analytic tools are all "created" by someone. In other words there is no such thing as a "natural" tool. Someone might say: "Just let the text say what it says and leave it alone." The problem with this statement is that every text is approaching us from a particular perspective. Also our experiences, prejudices, biases and ignorance tend to hinder us from totally understanding any text's original perspective. Psycholinguists, who study how the brain interacts with symbolic phenomena, have clearly demonstrated that what we bring to the text from our world-view, experiences, etc., affects what we think the original text says. Thus we are always "interpreting from a perspective" whenever we do literary analysis by the methods we use even if unaware. Therefore it is impossible to "just let a text speak" without other influences!

Thus, any set of descriptive tools will provide certain descriptive characteristics that work in certain limited ways. "Work" means they will give us perspectives that are plausible, intuitive, descriptive, reflective, and holistic. "Plausible" in the sense that our perspectives will be reasonable. "Intuitive" means that our analysis can be readily accessible and understood. "Descriptive" means attending to and portraying what is going on at various levels from various perspectives. "Reflective" means allowing a constant "mirror" that will expose our strategies and presuppositions in our analysis. "Holistic" means giving us a well rounded analysis within our chosen focus. These qualities will allow us to analyze and describe a text with a high degree of competence. One can always add more descriptive tools to enrich an analysis. The main thing is to know where our tools come from and then know their limitations. These two aspects of descriptive analysis will help us to know how much we understand, and how much to trust our analysis.

The five philosophic domains we have chosen to help us understand and describe liberation theology come from semantics, phenomenology, hermeneutics, semiotics, and structuralism. Except for the type of semantics we've chosen these systems of thought are based in the same type of European philosophy that influenced early liberation theologians in their university training. Now for a brief overview of each of this domains follows.

Semantics

"Meaning" is the central concern in semantics, but defining meaning is difficult.[2] Aspects like perspectives, deep structure vs. surface structure, and experience, all complicate any attempt to define meaning. For our purposes the definition of meaning will be contextually based. This means that meaning will be determined according to various interpretations within the context of various perspectives. For example, the classical hermeneutic tool works by allowing the grammatical arrangement of the text to be the boundaries for determining the linguistic meaning. Thus, we will find declarative propositions, and propositions that support, defend, or clarify the main propositions. The grammatical arrangement will dictate to us which propositions are declarative, or supportive, etc. Thus, we can say that according to the given context of the grammar, cultural context, and the writer this text has this "meaning."

Semantics will help us to "listen" to the classic case for liberation theology. The method we are going to use to do this is a modified form of a semantic structural analysis (SSA) used in linguistics. SSA assumes that meaning is always structured, and not random and inaccessible. The goal is to determine the structural system that carries the meaning of a text.[3] Then when we find the semantic structure we label the various structural elements. Semantic labeling is a very powerful tool,[4] and it operates in the following way: The proposition, "I love my wife, because she is kind," can be semantically labelled as:

Main Prop.------> I love my wife
Reason ----> She is kind

Finding and labeling propositions will allow us specifically to plot the reasoning and perspectives in liberation theology from the classical hermeneutic perspective. This tool will also help us to manage the data, and it provides a nice spring board out of the "classical hermeneutic" into our other perspectives. We will use this tool to specifically plot Gutierrez' classic book: A Theology of Liberation.

PHENOMENOLOGY

Edmund Husserl was the father of the phenomenological movement; he developed the phenomenological method, and every phenomenologist has retained at least some of his ideas.[5]   Thus, even though the phenomenological movement is quite diverse, Husserl is still a good representative for us to use in this study. Husserl (1859-1938) saw the need to return to rationality in the type of science practiced during his era. Scientists were positing their findings as "fact," thus failing to realize the limitations of their findings. In essence they were confusing the object of their investigation with the consciousness of it. In other words, they reified, or objectified, the object of their study. They did this by using methods, such as mathematics, to number, quantify, and measure the phenomena they were studying. They posited that the measurement of the object was the object, and by doing so they ushered in the era of positivistic science. Husserl's objection was that this was an irrational position because the "things themselves" were being violated by the methods of analysis because in essence they were "perspectivistic." For example, the weight, color, and shape of a chair is "essentially" different from the chair. In other words, the chair is more than its color, size, and shape, but positivistic science did not want to recognize this point.

... Husserl felt that there was too much concern in philosophy with concepts, and too little with data. He argued that philosophy had taken the data for granted, and had fallen into the habit of beginning uncritically with a set of concepts and making theory the result of a logical juggle with these. ... Back to the things themselves [became Husserl's motto] ...[6]

Husserl attempted to bring science back into rationality with phenomenology. Basically, phenomenology is a science of experience in which conscious experience is posited as the only valid description of anything that is "known."[7] Thus, a formal definition could be:

> Phenomenology is a self-critical methodology for reflexively examining and describing the lived evidence (the phenomena) which provides a crucial link in our philosophical and scientific understanding of the world.[8]

Phenomenology works by "bracketing" a phenomenon, which involves excluding a-priori assumptions about reality in the description of that phenomenon. This bracketing allows one to investigate and describe the actual lived world.

> We put out of action the general thesis which belongs to the essence of the natural standpoint, we place in brackets whatever it includes respecting the nature of Being: this entire natural world therefore which is continually "there for us," "present to our hand," and will ever remain there, is a "fact-world" of which we continue to be conscious, even though it pleases us to put it in brackets.[9]

This bracketing allows us to concentrate on how a phenomenon presents itself to our consciousness. The idea is to keep presuppositions which are outside the brackets from influencing the description of the phenomenon. The next step is to exclude all aspects that are not actually a part of the phenomena being examined. And the last step is to "specify the meaning that is essential in the reduction and description of the conscious experience being investigated."[10] For example, If we want to describe the essential characteristics of a chair we would bracket the natural attitude of quantification such as the shape, size, and color so that the essential characteristics are revealed. Focusing on the chair, we then would try to exclude everything from our perception of the chair in order to determine its essential characteristics. The last step would be to describe our findings.

The above is only a brief sketch of what phenomenology is and how it is used.   It is not in the scope of this chapter to perform a phenomenological description due to the amount of time this process requires.   Yet, a brief concrete example of the utility of this method is clearly demonstrated in the linguistic concept of the fundamental phoneme. In essence, the fundamental phoneme came about as a result of a radical shift in method for doing linguistic field work.   Instead of trying to mold every language into a Sanskrit, Greek, and Latin grammatical structures, linguists from the Prague School decided to focus on each language as a unique system.   This "bracketing" of the traditional way of doing linguistics eventually led to the discovery of the "phoneme." The phoneme is the most basic building block of verbal speech.[11]   This discovery revolutionized linguistics, and has become a very useful device in accurately representing language systems.   Thus, bracketing the natural attitude has proven to be a powerful tool.

Our application of phenomenology will only consist of using the practice of "bracketing" along with the concept of critically examining the way phenomena presents themselves to our consciousness.   These two "extractions" from phenomenology will prove to be extremely powerful in generating insight and description of liberation theology.   A brief analysis of Marxism and Christianity using "bracketing" will demonstrate how texts are re-organized by using this method.

PHENOMENOLOGICAL ANALYSIS OF MARXISM & CHRISTIANITY

Marx is said to have given Christianity an eidetic analysis, which is a critique focused on the actual practice of Christianity as it is manifested in the lived experience.   Phenomenology as a method was not readily available for Marx to use as a perspective, but his "naked looking" into the actual manifestation of Christianity as it is practiced, follows along similar lines as the "eidetic," or actual, experience of phenomena used in phenomenological analysis.   Marx bypassed religious texts and focused on the actual practice of "religion" on earth.   By looking at Christianity from a "praxis" standpoint, which is concerned with how its theory is actually practiced, Marx was able to give it a "this-world" critique.   This type of critique allowed him to negate, or reject, Christianity because he found it to be a massive oppressive force on earth. Oppressive in creating sectarian societies, and class distinctions such as clergy vs. laymen, and saved vs. unsaved, and in creating a symbol system that prohibited the people from taking concrete action to change their situation on earth.   The following is an "eidetic" perspective and comparison of Marxism and Christianity.

Phenomenology allows us to bracket doctrine with the use of the "epoche" in order to compare the practice of Marxism and Christianity on a broader "praxis" level. Basically, we're going to do a very simple bracket of both movements so that their sign function on a higher level can clearly be revealed. That is, both Marxism and Christianity will be bracketed to see what is metatextually happening with the propositions of each movement. Metatextuality simply refers to how a text functions from a multitude of perspectives outside of its immediate contextual boundaries. Remember, a text is simply a symbolic phenomena that can be read (see the semiotic section below). For example, Marxism is a text, or a movement, a literature, a world-view, that functions along side of many texts, comprised of other movements, literatures, world-views.

The following is a very simple "reading" of both texts, (a metatextual reading), in order to determine what they do in practice. For example, if I say; "open the door," I can focus on the words in the utterance, or focus on what they do. Focusing on what they do reveals that they can be looked on as a commandment, order, request, etc. Instead of focusing on the uttered words we are going to focus on what they point to. This is how we are going to examine Marxism and Christianity. The only phenomenology involved here is the "epoche," or bracketing, of doctrine. Doctrine will only be discussed as a sign that signals what is going on metatextually. Thus, the following will be a very elementary account of what the signs of both movements signify.

Christianity and Marxism both perspectivize the world. Marxism posits a "this-world-alone" position, which puts the known world as the source of criteria for analyzing and evaluating social structures. It rejects "other-worldly" or "non-material" assumptions as a source of alienation.

In contrast, Jesus taught about "this-world" and "the-other-world." The two worlds are the strongholds of power for the opposing spiritual forces of good and evil. Satan is temporally in charge of earth. Yahweh, the originator of all life, is in charge of heaven, the other world, where His will is perfectly performed.

Both perspectivize the cosmos. Marxism focuses on this earth as the center of what can be known. It does not allow for metaphysical ideologies to overrule actual lived practice on earth. Any other-worldly ideas used to justify any practice on earth are viewed as sources of oppression.

Yet, Jesus addresses both earth and heaven. He posited earth as an oppressive & fallen place where God by His own sovereign will does not dwell with all power yet. Heaven is the place where He does dwell with all power. Jesus pointed to an everlasting life in heaven where all oppressive factors are eliminated, such as death, oppression, Satan, etc.

Both perspectivize people. Marxism considers humanity in society the center of life on earth, thus he wants social structures that work toward this position. The individual is not the focus, rather it is the individual "in society." It posits that the material conditions are the single most important aspects determining how people arrange themselves on earth; moreover, it contends that material factors are the major influence on the way people's consciousness are formed.

Jesus posits people, and specifically the individual, as the center of his ministry. People are created in God's image, have inherent worth, and have an eternal spiritual nature. He has a long series of teachings related to how His individual followers are to treat people. Every person is said to be held responsible by Him in all aspects of life, which means He judges everyone according to their actions, including such aspects as motivations, attitudes, and values. "Love your neighbor as yourself" is His basic teaching concerning individual relationships.

Both desire justice for the oppressed. Marxism wants to eliminate private property, which is anti-social, for a social ownership and sharing of resources that will be of benefit to all people in society. Justice consists of eliminating the economic arrangement whereby people gain and maintain wealth at the expense of other people's labor power, and in establishing a social ownership of land and its resources.

Jesus provides individual justice that saves the person from sin and the destruction it produces such as the wrath of God. Operating from an Old Testament concept of a fallen human state resulting from Adam and Eve's disobedience in the garden of Eden, Jesus establishes a new order that satisfies God's justice requirements and enrolls individuals in an eternal heavenly kingdom freed from all the evils afflicting the present earth. The manifestation of Jesus' kingdom in the heart and mind of believers seems to be the main strategy for social justice as transformed people will transform society as they live out God's will on earth.

Both use a historical development model. Marxism bases his theory of social hierarchy on historical consciousness. Feudal society being a lower level society, a higher level would be capitalism and a higher level yet would be socialism and communism. Marx traces these types of social structures from the beginning of history to the present, and posits more advanced societies replacing outdated ones.

Jesus uses the Old Testament to trace His "history" from the creation to the end of the world. The basic theme follows the fall of people from God's presence due to disobedience, and God's redeeming activity to restore communion with them. The final form of society is posited as the culmination of this restoration activity in the new heavenly kingdom where all is restored in perfection after the second return of Christ on earth.

Both target and attack an enemy. Marxism verbally attacks social structures that alienate and oppress. Lists like private property, class divisions, metaphysical ideologies like Christianity and political institutions that generate class distinctions as the enemies of humanity.

Jesus attacks Satan, the main enemy of God, and rebellious and sinful attitudes of people that lead to selfish ambition, greed, lust, murder, every form of dehumanizing activity, unbelief and physical death.

Both strive for a more human world. Marxism wants to establish a new order of material existence in which people can fully develop without oppression.

Jesus wants His followers to exemplify redeemed behavior that concretely manifests itself in behavior that is human, free, responsible, and abundant. "Love others as oneself" is the type of behavior Jesus teaches.

The above bracketing of doctrine conducted with the limited use of phenomenological epoche lays out a broad dialogue base that will serve us in understanding the ways that liberation theologians have interacted with Marxist texts. Backing away from specific doctrine allows the possibility of reflecting on what is happening at other levels. This is exactly the type of influence that European philosophical systems like phenomenology have on liberation thinkers. In essence, they take a "perspective" like poverty and then re-enter a text and "re-write" theology according to the new paradigm. This basically changes both the paradigm used and the theology that is re-written. The next section on hermeneutics further shows how easily paradigms can change theology depending on what perspective is used by the theologian.

HERMENEUTICS

Hermeneutics is an age old discipline which has evolved into different forms throughout the centuries. The Greek god "Hermes" was said to be the one to interpret the messages of the gods, and then present them to the people in an intelligible way.

Hermes transmitted the message of the gods to the mortals, that is to say, he not only announced them verbatim but acted as "interpreter" who renders their words intelligible - and meaningful - which may require some point of clarification or other, additional, commentary. Hermeneutics is consequently engaged in two tasks: one, the ascertaining of the exact meaning-content of a word, sentence, text, etc.; two, the discovery of the instructions contained in symbolic forms.[12]

The above is a good account of the "classical" notion of hermeneutics. Classical hermeneutics, or the grammatical historical method, is still the standard used in evangelical circles today. It provides a "normative" account of language which keeps the interpreters feet on the floor and standardizes boundaries for reasonable guidelines in exegesis. Yet, this philosophy has shifted its aims over the years. Thus, the classical aim of determining the exact meaning of a text has now shifted into many different brands of hermeneutics.

Modern hermeneutics is an outgrowth of phenomenology. One of Husserl's students was Martin Heidegger. As stated earlier, phenomenology wanted to bring science back into rationality by escaping the natural attitude through the use of self-critical methodologies in describing phenomena. In Husserl's quest for a "pure" science, one which he thought was possible only through examination of one's conscious experience of phenomena, he ended up in a radical no-man's land that proved to have little utility for practical living. Heidegger spotted "the irrealism of Husserl's project," and made a radical departure from Husserl's "pure phenomenology."[13]

In essence, Heidegger changed the focus from the Husserlian quest of finding a pure descriptive method, to a more "ontological" question which explores how people arrive at understanding from "being-in-the-world."

Heidegger is not, therefore, concerned with a method which - once designed - could be learned and employed by professional hermeneuticians to resolve their conflicts of interpretation. Heidegger has little, if anything, to tell all those who want to know why they ought to prefer one particular interpretation to another. Instead, he painstakingly explores the ontological foundations of the understanding which men and women reach by the very fact of being-in-the-world. This understanding is a necessity, rather than an exceptional achievement; a necessity constantly arising from their very existence, as this existence stubbornly and incessantly reveals to them the variety of possibilities in which they might be-in-the-world.[14]

Starting with Heidegger's fundamental redefinition of Husserl's project hermeneutics has taken a variety of new arrangements. For example, Bleicher has identified three distinguishable types of hermeneutical inquiry; "hermeneutical theory, hermeneutical philosophy, and critical hermeneutics."[15]   Basically, hermeneutical theory seeks "relatively objective" knowledge in the classical sense. One of the key ingredients of this strand is that language is in relationship, which is to say that context determines the meaning. Our Semantic Structural Analysis (SSA) of Gutierrez' A Theology of Liberation follows this strand of hermeneutics. The SSA simply arranges a text according to the semantic levels the information belongs, thus a "classical" hermeneutic.

Yet hermeneutic philosophy rejects the idea that we can know exact meaning because the interpreter always plays a significant role in generating meaning. In other words, the traditional foundations of knowledge are only "ways-of-looking" at phenomenon, and thus they keep us from being able to give pure and unbiased renditions of meaning.

Then critical hermeneutics posits "extra-linguistic" factors of "work and domination," such as economic institutions and power structures, as significant contexts for the shaping of human consciousness.

> ... Habermas arrive[s] at ... [his] critical hermeneutics which combines a methodical and objective approach with the striving for practically relevant knowledge. "Critical" should here be taken to mean mainly the appraisal of existing states of affairs in view of standards that derive from the knowledge of something better that already exists as a potential or a tendency in the present; it is guided by the principle of Reason as the demand for unrestricted communication and self-determination. More specifically, this epithet should indicate an affinity with both the "critical theory" of the Frankfurt School and with Marx's work. Their legacy is the exhortation to change reality rather than merely interpret it.[16]

It should begin to be clear that our representative selections from hermeneutics stem from their utility for interpreting liberation theology. We have seen how the integrated work of the Frankfurt School played a central role in the development and practice of liberation theologians in Latin America. In other words, the type of hermeneutics used plays a very significant role in the theological debates among liberation theologians and those who oppose them. The various approaches of hermeneutics have also played a very significant role in the theological schools in the United States and Europe. It is safe to say that the three strands of hermeneutics represented in this short review are prevalent in the theological arena of Protestant and Catholic circles worldwide. We will use all three of them in our analysis of liberation theology.

SEMIOTICS

Semiotics is a study of signs, which are representations that point to various meanings, and how meaning is attributed to them. Eco defines semiotics as:

Semiotics is concerned with everything which can be taken as a sign. A sign is everything which can be taken as significantly substituting for something else.[17]

Saussure and Peirce are considered the founders of this particular field of study in the 20th century,[18] but the concept of semiotics has been evident from the beginning of creation. In Genesis 2:19-20 God empowered the first person to "name" the creation, to give a verbal symbol to represent elements of the environment. Thus, semiotics is an old concept, yet recently it has contributed to our understanding of the enormous complexity surrounding the notion of a "sign and its signified." The result of this investigation has proved to be an oasis for descriptive method and analysis.

Semiotic based methods empower with a host of tools to be used with anything faintly related to symbolism. From basic speech utterance, where the act of naming is a strategic choice from other possibilities, to the clothes we wear, which are non-verbal phenomena that point to something beyond itself. With unlimited analysis possibilities, the semiotic method is a very powerful tool.

The semiotic method consists of creatively employing the following concepts: Sign, which consists of the signified and signifier; paradigmatic and syntagmatic; synchronic and diachronic analysis; and assorted concepts like reader, text, intertextuality, and metatextuality. A very brief explanation of these concepts follows.

Sign refers to anything that points beyond itself like Castro's beard that equates him with Cuba's revolution. Signified is the meanings attributed to signs. Signifier is the sound image of a word. For example, the verbal utterance of "dog" is a signifier which means a four footed hairy animal, which is the signified. The structural relationship between the signifier and the signified constitutes a linguistic sign. Syntagmatic refers to the horizontal aspect of symbolic phenomena. For example, the linear denotation of the actual utterance in speech. Paradigmatic refers to the vertical aspect of symbolic phenomena. For example, the levels of possible connotative meaning placed upon the linear denotation of an utterance. Synchronic analyzes something by the way it functions during a specific time period regardless of how it operated in the past or future. Diachronic refers to the "historical" aspect of language phenomena, such as documenting language change over time. Now let us clarify the individual concepts.

Reader refers to "those-who-interpret" the signs of their experience. In essence, a reader is a person who interprets the meaning to signs. Text refers to any phenomena that operates as a system of signification. Intertextuality is the notion that every text is in relation with other texts, and that there is no text outside of this relationship. Metatextuality is the notion that texts can be analyzed according to how they function outside of their immediate textual boundaries. For example, the gender roles of greeting can be seen as signaling a superior/inferior relationship from a metatextual analysis. In other words, a greeting could be analyzed according to the words uttered, but a metatextual analysis would look at how the whole utterance signals dominance or submission.

The brief description above of semiotic concepts can be thought of as "ways-of-looking" at texts. Each concept offers a unique perspective as the brief explanations above demonstrate. As a unit of analysis, the semiotic approach serves as a very effective tool for analyzing any symbolic phenomena.[19] For example, the synchronic analysis will allow us to view the Catholic Church's attitude at any point in time we want, and the diachronic analysis will allow us to trace the evolution of liberation theology over time. Another example would be the metatextual analysis of how the texts of the left and right wings of the Protestant and Catholic churches, the Pope, Marxism, and the poor people of Latin America, all signify different meanings outside the boundaries of their own specific contexts. For Example, Gustavo Gutierrez can be looked upon as a hero by the poor people of Latin America, and as a heretic by the Pope. Looking at how texts communicate outside their boundaries will give us a much fuller picture of what is happening, and a sharper analysis of liberation rhetoric.

STRUCTURALISM

Structuralism is a philosophical assumption about the world, and about the way people organize their perceptions. The notion of "people organizing" is a structuralist notion that posits human nature as a structuring nature, which means humans strive to see things in recognizable patterns.[20] Many of the structuralist notions come from an "Italian jurist

Giambattista Vico." In The New Science published in 1725, Vico claimed that people create myths to live by, and in turn these mythical structures, after they are established, serve to organize society.[21]   In essence, mythical structures pre-figure the way the world is perceived.   For example, the notions of good and evil are a result of mythical structures that persuade people to view phenomenon as good and evil. For instance, when we say that murder is an evil act, it is because society places a high priority on human life, but if we de-value human life, then murder could become a good thing. Thus, seeing the world in categories of good and evil is a result of the structuring process at work within societies.

Jean Piaget attempted to define the fundamental characteristics of structuralism on the ideas of wholeness, transformation, and self-regulation.[22] "Wholeness" simply refers to a system that maintains itself; for example, a basic biological cell has its own internal network within its boundaries that allow elements in or out of its system. "Transformation" refers to the non-static living nature of structures, which means they transform into different modes of being at different times. "Self-regulation" refers to the internal mechanism of self-maintenance such as the social rules operating to keep a cultural system alive, or the linguistic rules of a language that allows its participants to operate within it.[23]

Structuralism is a "structural notion" that organizes our thinking about the world just as the creation of mythical structures eventually structure the "way-we-see." Some of the modern notions evolving from this movement are currently taken for granted among the academic community such as the notion of "process" among speech communication scholars, and the notion of "eco-systems" among anthropology scholars. The idea is that:

> ... the nature of every element in any given situation has no significance by itself, and in fact is determined by its relationship to all the other elements involved in that situation. In short, the full significance of any entity or experience cannot be perceived unless and until it is integrated into the structure of which it forms a part.[24]

From this notion of "interrelatedness" the poststructuralist school studies the language phenomena of society to determine how the existing structural elements are used to empower some at the expense of others.[25] Thus, poststructuralism assumes the interrelatedness of language with social structures.   The difference is that the motivations for this type of structuralist research is for ideological reasons, as the purpose is to expose structures in order to change undesirable elements contained within them. Structural oppression can result from a naive society being blind to the effect of the symbol systems operating in society.

>The second branch of structuralism, perhaps more properly called poststructuralism, is ideological in orientation. It combines the anti-empirical methodology of classical structuralism with ideas derived from Marxism, psychoanalysis and philosophy, to analyze cultural institutions, such as literature, as mediation to ideologies.[26]

Thus, poststructuralism is used as a critical methodology for exposing power structures in order to change undesirable elements of them. Liberation theologians have adopted the poststructuralistic motivation for critiquing structures in societies. As a result, many of these theologians are attempting to re-write history in order to expose the oppression that language symbol systems have had on the global community.

We will extract from structuralism the idea of "wholeness," or "interrelatedness," the idea of "transformation," and the poststructuralist's method of critiquing power structures in societies. The reason for adopting poststructuralism's ideological critique is simply due to the fact that this is exactly what liberation theologians are doing to the societies in which they live. Wholeness is used because of its utility for outlining the skeleton of a movement within its system. This will help us plot the rhetorical aspects of liberation theology in a clear fashion, thus keeping our focus clear at every step. And "transformation" is used because it will help us to determine how liberation theologians are attempting to manipulate the "deep-structure" of the eco-structure in order to create the effect they desire.

Conclusion

Each of the philosophic domains above and the tools gleaned from them give us particular ways at looking at liberation theology. Each tool has limitations and problems. For example, using a full blown phenomenological method would give us a very narrow analysis that some would say is unrealistic and abstract. Yet by using specific tools from a combination of the philosophic domains gives us the opportunity of a fuller view of liberation theology.

Now that we have a sufficient background in continental/European philosophy along with some analytic tools let us analyze some major liberation texts.

ANALYSIS

INTRODUCTION

We will start our analysis of liberation theology by outlining the propositions of Gustavo Gutierrez's book, A Theology of Liberation. This book "remains the best known work in liberation theology and the best overall statement of its position."[1] We will organize the propositions into discourse segments and label each segment according to the immediate syntactical context using a semantic structural analysis. We will also address other major texts of liberation theology, which will be drawn upon to fill out a complete pattern of this movement. These texts include the Pope, the official doctrine of the Vatican, Marxism, the poor people of Latin America, the Bible, the political structures of North and South America, and the left and right wings of the Catholic and Protestant Churches. Everything combined will provide an excellent introduction to liberation theology.

PROPOSITIONS OF LIBERATION THEOLOGY

We will bracket Gustavo Gutierrez's book A Theology of Liberation[2] with the classical hermeneutic perspective using our semantic structural analysis. We want to allow the syntactical context of Gutierrez's discourse to guide our interpretation. Thus, our first focus is on Gutierrez's book. We will outline the propositional structures and label these propositions according to what they signify in context. This will give us Gutierrez's arguments for establishing liberation theology. But the following propositional outline should not give the impression that Gutierrez writes in a straightforward manner which can be easily outlined. In fact, his writing style is similar to the way a spider builds a web,[3] which means our propositions are an attempt to provide an outline of his statements. Admittedly, the outline may violate some of the intricate meanings he intended. But we hope to compensate for any possible misrepresentation of his thoughts by drawing on a host of other liberation theology publications to clarify our schematic treatment of Gutierrez's work. Thus, the following outline represents the main propositions found in the four sections of Gutierrez's book.

Five propositions contain the major tenets of liberation theology expressed in A Theology of Liberation. In essence we are going to bracket each proposition in order to analyze them within their own propositional context. This will serve us in structuring our analysis, and it will keep things clear during the analysis. Now let us start with our first proposition.

PROPOSITION ONE: Theology is constantly changing.

A. Reason: Theological reflection is natural.

i. Justification: Every believer follows "some" theology, and it's evident that anyone who has "accepted" a faith system has at least thought about how their faith reflects on their actual lived experience.

B. Example: Classical Theology concerned itself with "spiritual growth," which consisted of gaining spiritual wisdom and implementing it in daily life. It operated off of a Platonic absolute, and this absolute was considered the most important aspect in life. The present life was considered to be "contingent," thus it was not valued as much as the absolute.

C. Example: From the 12th century on, theology became a "science," an intellectual discipline, born of the meeting of faith and reason. The focus was to systematize theology so that everything fit neatly into a package, and in clear exposition of this systematization.

i. Evidence: Works of Thomas Aquinas, and the Council of Trent demonstrate this "shift."

D. Example: Presently, theology is a critical reflection on praxis, which manifests itself in actual individual and economic Christian practice based on doctrine. Concern for "charity," which is the commitment to God and neighbor, demonstrates this shift. This shift follows the Biblical emphasis for being concerned about how we treat others. A faith centered in the service of all people.

i. Evidence: Vatican Council II reaffirmed the idea of a Church of service and not of power.

ii. Evidence: The emphasis of human action as the point of departure for all reflection, which is a Marxist notion focused on actual practice based on theory, and it is geared to the transformation of the world. All activity is reflected on to determine if the activity violates theory, or vice versa, for the purpose of liberating the church from being alienating.

iii. Evidence: A calling of the Church to be politically active by attempting to make the world a better place for everyone.

ANALYSIS OF PROPOSITION ONE

Gutierrez opens dialogue with us concerning theology, liberation, and development. The first proposition strategically sets up later claims. For example, the first proposition states that theology is constantly changing because theological reflection is a natural activity that many Christians do. By positing an ongoing evolution of theology Gutierrez subtly allows himself to proceed with reflecting on theology in Latin America in light of the current evolution of theology. But, the kind of reflection he proceeds with is quite different from someone simply figuring out how to practice the Christian faith in the lived-world. In essence, Gutierrez is arguing for a radical theology based on the common phenomenon of people thinking about out how to practice their faith in their lived-world. But, he uses this example to embark on a theology-building journey that is quite uncommon, as it is rare for someone to create a completely new theology by re-arranging and articulating a new global theology called liberation theology. Thus, this first proposition "empowers" him to begin his theological reflection; yet it is accomplished by mixing a natural everyday reflective type of behavior with a highly strategic theology building event.[4]

Also, this seemingly benign move of granting himself permission to do theological reflection begins a transformational process that will challenge the usual theologian vs. laymen distinction within established church hierarchies. Liberation theologians want a community effort in theology building and practice, thus they desire more laymen participation in creating and doing theology. They believe that "Biblical interpretation is best done by people in mission thinking and acting communally."[5] Thus, Gutierrez wants community involvement in theology making, and he wants to dis-empower the theology-producing church hierarchy by giving more authority to "laypeople" within the Catholic Church.

As one might expect, those who favor the hierarchical arrangement in the church do not want everyone involved in making theology for several reasons. One of the most important reasons for resisting more laity participation in theology making is to keep a minority empowered with the power of "voice." Yet liberation theologians want more people taking an active part in the decisions that affect their life because they feel that communities without voice are vulnerable to the whims of those in power. Leonardo Boff, a Brazilian liberation theologian writes:

> Christians are steeped in venerable traditions, ... and forms of power - all powerfully controlled and centralized by a body of experts, the hierarchy. ... A bishop may decide to halt a project that affects priests, religious, pastoral leaders, and dozens of communities. Without any previous discussion, he may literally expel religious leaders from his diocese and dismiss the lay leaders, having the faith community confused. There is no one to whom they can appeal because they are dealing with the final judge.[6]

Thus, community involvement in theological decisions are threatening to those who have been used to dictating theology. And this threat is a result of liberation theologians who want to empower laymen with the authority and responsibility of all the aspects of their faith.

After Gutierrez neatly allows himself the opportunity to embark on theological reflection, with a because-it-is-natural argument, he lays a foundation stone for his liberation theology by stating that "theology is always changing." He eventually wants to say that since theology always changes, liberation theology is the current historical manifestation of that change. This is an attempt to naturalize his new theology, to make his theology appear to be a natural and inevitable consequence of history. His diachronic analysis of Christian theology, in which he traces changes in theology over time, identifies individuals who change theology after reflecting on the current philosophy of their time. He uses examples to justify this position such as the Platonic absolute establishing the foundation of classical theology. These examples strengthen Gutierrez's historical argument that theology has changed in every century due to "someone" re-contextualizing the faith. Thus, Gutierrez wants the new manifestation of this natural historical transformation process to be liberation theology.

The idea of "transformation" will help us here in our analysis of re-contextualizing the faith. Gutierrez implies that in every age someone comes up with a unique philosophy that changes the focus and texture of the Christian faith. He wants to extend this notion so that a "new" set of philosophers and theologians can transform the faith again. Ideally, for Gutierrez the next change will move the Christian faith into the province of liberation theology. The new transformation will again re-contextualize the faith and, like Jesus threatening the established and obstinate Jewish religious leaders, status quo structures will resist in the fear that they may lose their place of power. Luis G. del Valle sums up this transformational tension with the following quote:

> Here, then, we have another feature of this new way of doing theology. It always involves a certain amount of tension with ecclesiastical authorities. This does not mean that we spurn their role as pastors. It does mean that the loyalty of Christians will be a critical-minded one; for they will gradually assume their own full share of responsibility as Christians living in the world.[7]

Thus, the church hierarchy which wants to be in charge of all the decision-making among believers is threatened by a transformational process that wants to empower the laity with a voice.

Valle goes on to chart the specific transformation process that is competing over this issue of voice. He charts this process by using a source-message-receiver communication model.[8]

Element	Situation A	Situation B
sender	professors and books	historical reality, revelation & tradition
medium	classes and written materials	first-hand contact and experience, group reflection, tutorial, dialogue conferences, written materials
message	systematic philosophy	God's plan in salvation history
code	formal logic and deductive metaphysics	transcendental epistemology, logic, anthropology, metaphysics
referent	revelation and trad-ition;a certain way of comprehending being	God and human beings operating in history
receiver	the students	the whole work team: students, professors, and tutors

Notice, how the traditional system of "A" is in direct conflict with the liberation theology system "B." For example, the traditional sender is a professional theologian who imparted understanding to receivers who passively comprehended the message. System B seeks to shift this power away from the theologian to the present lived-experience, the revelation of the Biblical text, and the tradition of the church's teachings. In essence, this transformational process threatens to eliminate a "center," which in this case is a highly trained theologian, by empowering a "periphery," or the laity, with a critical-reflective method of arriving at theology in the present lived experience. As Valle's quote indicates, "tension" results from this process as the center wants to keep the power of voice, and the periphery wants to establish a voice in order to have more power to control their lives.

This transformation also seeks to establish a new center of Christian thought and theology, namely, in Latin America and in Africa as: "The power and decision-making centers of the Christian churches are still located in Europe and the United States."[9]   Many liberation theologians like Sergio Torres are predicting a de-Christianizing of the Western World with a new center of Christian theology located in the Third World. This shift would radically change the way theology is written due to the unique lived-experience of the Third World as one which basically consists of an oppressed people. Liberation theologians hope that this shift will humanize theology because the new centers of theology in the Third World will attempt to give emphasis to how the church treats human beings, something they believe the Western World and its churches have not considered. Liberation theology demonstrates this shift of humanizing theology with its emphasis upon the Second Greatest Commandment to "love ones neighbor as oneself" in the economic, social, political, and religious aspects of life.

In 1Dii of the outline Gutierrez identifies the type of theology that creates this tension with the center. It is a theology based on how the lived-experience reflects the Christian doctrine and vice versa. In other words, liberation theology talks about God in a different way. The traditional approach to theology talked about God by determining correct dogma from a classical hermeneutic interpretation of the Bible, and then teaches this interpretation as the way to follow God. Liberation theology reflects on the lived experience then goes to the Bible to figure out how theology pertains to the lived condition. Gutierrez explains this further.

> Liberation theology would say that God is first contemplated and practiced, and only then thought about. What we mean by this is that worshipping God and doing his will are the necessarSwcondition for thinking about him. Only on the basis of mysticism and practice

is it possible to work out an authentic and respectful way of speaking about God. ... Contemplation and involvement in history are two essential and interrelated dimensions of Christian life. The mystery is revealed in contemplation and in solidarity with the poor: this is what we call the first act or step. Christian life; only after this can this life inspire a process of reasoning: this is the second act or step.[10]

Gutierrez provides the following chart to demonstrate this "new" way of doing theology:

First step	Second step
Contemplation	Theology
Practice	Speaking
Silence	

Gutierrez argues that this kind of "being" theology reflects the emphasis of the first Christian community as recorded in the New Testament book of Acts. This community was referred to as the "The Way" in Acts 9:2. Gutierrez traces the Greek work "hodos," which is translated as "way," as referring to conduct and life style. In essence, his argument states that following Jesus requires doing theology in the totality of the lived-experience in such a manner that "Christians are distinguished by a behavior, a life style."[11] Thus, for Gutierrez, the "new" method of liberation theology is actually an old first principle of the Christian faith.

Essentially, liberation theology calls the economic, social, political, and religious structures of the global community to reflect the "love-your-neighbor-as-yourself" commandment. In 1Diii, Gutierrez says this must be accomplished in the total lived-experience, which includes the church becoming politically active. The great commission given by Jesus to "make disciples of all nations" found in Matthew chapter 28 is to be carried out by declaring the death, burial, and resurrection of the Savior in the midst of poverty, injustice, and alienation. This is carried out by both contemplating "that everything comes from the gratuitous love of the Father," and by prophetically denouncing "the situation -- and its structural causes -- of injustice and robbery in which the poor of Latin America live."[12] The notion of theological evolution emphasizes that the "biblical religion is a historical faith, and that the challenge of our times is to change society through self-conscious intentional action."[13]

Frederick Herzog, Professor of Systematic Theology at Duke University Divinity School, examines the new hermeneutic liberation theologians use in writing their theology. In essence, the Bible is viewed as a proclamation "from a poverty text to poverty context."[14] The Biblical writers proclaimed the poverty of a suffering Messiah, sent to save a suffering and oppressed human race, and they proclaimed this under the ethos of being voluntary slaves to their Lord. This "poverty context" is the new context of liberation theology. In essence, theology is written from the viewpoint of the poor, or suffering, in the spiritual, economic, social, and political arenas. Extending the poverty context into the entire lived-experience is one of the distinguishing marks of liberation theology.

Gutierrez urges support for this new hermeneutic that allows a theological extension of the poverty context into the economic, social, and political realms by claiming that liberation theology will eventually become the dominant theology.

> ... just as people were once molded by Greek thought. Those who cling to the old ways of thinking, who resist the new approach and accuse its proponents of distorting the faith, remind us of those who once opposed the use of Aristotle's philosophy in theology. And like the latter, they really have no future.[15]

This bold and confident statement demonstrates the seriousness and strong commitment of liberation theologians. They are seeking an intricate relationship between the heavenly kingdom-of-God, the lived world, and the church. Leonardo Boff explains this relationship with the following quote.

> [The kingdom] is the utopia that is realized in the world, the final good of the whole of creation in God, completely liberated from all imperfection and penetrated by the Divine. The world is the arena for the historical realization of the Kingdom. Presently the world is decadent and stained by sin; because of this, the Kingdom of God is raised up against the powers of the anti-Kingdom, engaged in the onerous process of liberation so that the world might accept the Kingdom itself and thus achieve its joyous goal. The Church is that part of the world that, in the strength of the Spirit, has accepted the Kingdom made explicit in the person of Jesus Christ, the Son of God incarnated in oppression. It preserves the constant memory and consciousness of the Kingdom, celebrating its presence in the world, shaping the way it is proclaimed, and at the service of the world. The Church is not the Kingdom but rather its sign (explicit symbol)

and its instrument (mediation) in the world.[16]

This relationship of heavenly ideals with both the world and the church contains the essential components of how liberation theology wants the church to become politically active. In essence, the Kingdom of God, by working through the church, is to struggle against "anti-Kingdom" forces until the world submits by accepting total liberation. This desire to Christianize the world's economic, social, political, and religious structures stems from a secularization of the second coming to earth by Jesus Christ, which the New Testament posits as a phenomenon that will occur in future history. Liberation theologians believe that this second coming is metaphorical, and that God always intended the church to implement His ideals in the world in such a way that the principles of the heavenly kingdom would be practiced on earth. In 1Diii Gutierrez calls the church into the political realm. This extension of God's liberation into the political realm is meant to facilitate the secularization of the kingdom of God on earth.

Yet, a paradigmatic analysis of this attempt to make the church a political entity gives another interpretation. This move to extend the Christian notion of salvation, or liberation, from personal sin into the entire spectrum of life could easily be interpreted as a failing church's attempt to be legitimate in a society "waning of Christian vitality."[17] Gutierrez wants to incorporate Christian principles into the total lived-experience because he believes that this is the proper thing to do in order to represent the genuine spirit of Christianity. But, the church has always been politically active even though at times it has not been consciously aware of it. Yet Gutierrez is calling the church into the political arena in a way that seeks to incorporate Christian principles into the economic, social, and political spheres of life.

No Christian group has so radically attempted to do this, so why would Gutierrez want to be so radical? He says that it is a desire to be authentically Christian because the incorporation of heavenly principles into the total lived-experience is the only way to follow Jesus. Yet, Jesus only called His disciples into this type of radical living, and there is not one New Testament reference where Jesus ever commands unbelievers to follow His teachings when they have not first believed in Him. Plus, it is very questionable whether the type of Christianity that Gutierrez advocates is similar to the Founder's.[18] Gutierrez is clearly outside the immediate contextual interpretation of the Bible when he calls for the economic, social, and political structures to adopt Christian principles. The question is why does Gutierrez do this?

We have already alluded to the possibility of the church seeking to be more legitimate in the world by attempting to place Gospel ideals under the foundation of the total lived-experience.   Even though this is a possibility, it seems to me that the liberation theologians of the Third World have witnessed so much suffering caused by poor economic, social, and political systems that they are searching for a solution that will reverse the structures that produce this suffering.   The call to make the church more political is an attempt to "do something" in their lived-experience that will make a difference in the quality of life for those who live in Latin America. Thus a drowning man grasps for any rope that seems to offer life.

Phenomenological bracketing allows us to see the overwhelming consciousness formation of poverty.   It is safe to say that if the cold, cruel, and de-humanizing reality of poverty did not exist in the Third World sectors of our planet, then liberation theology would never have gotten out of the theological arm chairs of its proponents.   The epoche or bracket on poverty in liberation theology reformats all thoughts and assumptions of this new world-view.   Thus, poverty is the single biggest hermeneutic tool used to re-contextualize the Christian faith into liberation theology.

In conclusion, Gutierrez allows himself to begin a new theological journey by using a natural reflective activity to justify re-contextualizing Christian theology.   This activity empowers the Catholic laity with a voice, and at the same time creates tension between the laity and the traditional Catholic Church hierarchy.   In essence, this re-contextualization talks about God in a different way.   Basically, the poverty context of the New Testament is extended into the economic, social, political, and religious structures, which results in a theology for the total lived-experience.   This is an attempt to make Christianity concrete in the Latin American context by eliminating poverty.

The next proposition will involve a political and economic evaluation of global economic, social, political, and religious structures.

PROPOSITION TWO: The world community is undergoing an unequal transformation that is producing massive wealth for a few and massive poverty for most, and this inequality must stop.

A. Rejected Solution: The strategy of "developmentalism," which posits that poor countries mimic the practices of the rich countries in order to catch up with them, is not acceptable.

i. Reason: Poor countries perceive that rich countries are rich due to practicing injustice and coercion, thus they do not want to mimic a fraudulent system.

ii. Reason: Past experience with developmentalism has not changed the social and economic conditions in Latin America. Because development never challenged the existing structural foundations due to the influence of large international economic powers, who were only interested in increasing their power base.

B. Desired Solution: The strategy of "liberation" is needed, which involves human freedom from everything that would restrict self-fulfillment.

i. Reason: Science has enabled man to alter his surroundings, and acquire genuine exterior and interior freedom. Also, historical processes are perceived as the genesis of consciousness of the liberation of man.

a. Evidence: Modern philosophers have contributed to this idea such as Descartes' idea that experience should conform to ones conception; Hegel's demand that everyone participate in all aspects of life affecting them; Marx's scientific understanding of historical reality; Freud's unconscious determinants that repressed human desire; and Marcuse's critique of the values espoused by society which oppressed all who followed them; all the above contributed to this idea in their philosophy.

ii. Reason: The Catholic Church since John XXIII has stressed the urgency of eliminating the existing injustices and the need for an economic development geared to the service of man.

a. Evidence: A Catholic documents such as the Populorum progressio speak of building a world where every man, no matter what his race, religion or nationality, can live a fully human life, freed from servitude imposed on him by other men or by natural forces over which he has not sufficient control.

b. Evidence: The Biblical message of Christ as liberator provides the framework for this liberation. In essence, "sin" is to refuse to love one's neighbor, thus refusing to love God. Thus, sin is the ultimate cause of poverty, injustice, and oppression, and it is behind social, economic, and religious structures that are oppressive.

ANALYSIS OF PROPOSITION TWO

Gutierrez rejects "developmentalism" in 3A because it hasn't worked in the past, and because it operates within a structure that is oppressive. The power of "voice" is again at stake here. The existing structures of developmentalism are considered fraudulent because they only perpetuate their own power base. In essence, development is not conducted in a manner that will allow Latin American people to choose freely among existing alternatives; rather all decision alternatives exist "within" existing structures that are in power. During an interview with Dow Kirkpatrick, a United Methodist missionary in Peru, concerning the issue of mutual dependence of the First World on the Third World and vice versa, Gutierrez and Javier Iguiniz responded with a concise statement concerning the fundamental notion of voice.

The problem is not who depends on whom. Rather, our countries decline or develop according to the rhythm of the needs of the developed nations. We have no possibility for making decisions about our own needs. Basic structural factors in the international economic system draw the parameters within which we must move. They come from the logic of world capitalism, whose dynamic pole, whose rhythm, is outside.[19]

Fundamentally, Gutierrez seeks to empower Latin America with a voice by creating independent economic, social, and political structures. Thus, the first step in doing this is to refuse to accept developmental strategies that only perpetuate First World domination of Third World peoples. Gutierrez doesn't mention the cultural and moral values in operation in Latin America that contribute to poverty. He only sees "outside" oppressive structures imposing their slavish ways on the poor. His desired solution is a liberation from everything that would restrict human self-fulfillment, yet it is outer rather than inner change that is targeted.[20] This transformational proposition would eliminate a situation in which a minority "center" dominated a majority "periphery." However, when Gutierrez was asked about the possibility of the majority becoming oppressors of the minority once they gained power, he responded: "But then at least we will take turns!"[21] He went on to say that no liberated nation has been as "massively and systematically reduced to conditions in which the poor live today" as in Latin America.

Gutierrez seems to be extremely naive with the last two responses concerning the outcome of the periphery gaining power, as it seems that he forgot to read about the violent human purging of the "other side" after the revolutions in China, Russia, and Vietnam. The poor in Latin America have their life, which is more than can be said of the twenty million peasants that froze and starved to death in just one winter of Russia's revolution. And if the majority of oppressed people within Latin America were given a voice, then Gutierrez should be giving some sort of indications of the type of society that will be manifested. Nazi Germany claimed to be "Christian," thus any tacit argument on Gutierrez's part that assumes "Christians" will be more benevolent towards the conquered seems to be an invalid assumption. Gutierrez needs to explain specifically how the new social structure he desires would operate in order to eliminate any doubts about how the majority would function once they gained power. Thus, the interview with Kirkpatrick gives little support to the goals of equality and power sharing, and Gutierrez seems to be naive and short-sighted in his answers. Yet, the fundamental notion behind the creation of a new society is the idea that humanity is in charge of and "capable of" creating social structures.

In 2Bi Gutierrez posits humans as the agents to change the way social structures are arranged. Rene De Visme Williamson calls this a "secularization" of religion, which means a "completely desacralized world."[22] This is a fundamental notion of liberation theology. Support for placing humans in charge of social structure creation and change is partially gained in the first proposition, which states that theology is always changing. Gutierrez's supplants the Biblical account and places humanity in charge of how the world is organized. Armed with science and Christian morality, Gutierrez seeks to create a new society. By placing the responsibility of creating social structure on humanity, Gutierrez has "secularized" the Biblical interpretations that God is in control of the way societies are arranged.

Metatextually, this secularization can be interpreted as a defense of God as it is extremely difficult to justify the proclamation of a just and righteous God who establishes and maintains governmental systems that are corrupt, manipulative, de-humanized, and coercive. Liberation theologians never openly admit to defending God, yet a metatextual interpretation clearly allows this interpretation.   In essence, the metatextual analysis allows one to read the discursive maneuvers of a text to determine how the speaker sets up a model reader with the appropriate instructions about how to realize a certain persuasive effect. For example, Umberto Eco details how Pliny the Younger built fame for himself by writing about Pliny the Elder's fate at the Mt. Vesuvius volcano.[23] Younger never admits to building fame for himself, but the net outcome of his description of Elder's heroic activity during the volcanic eruption gives him fame by association with Elder's heroic activity.

In a similar way, the net effect of Gutierrez's secularization, which places the responsibility of social structure creation on human shoulders, defends God from being held responsible for the corrupt governmental systems of Latin America. Gutierrez never says this, and he may not be aware of this interpretation, but the net effect of proposition 2Bi defends God from being the author of corrupt governments. Gutierrez can also be interpreted as defending God when he alludes to Hegel's notion that states: "what is rational is actual, and what is actual is rational"[24]; with the notion that "historical processes are perceived as the genesis of consciousness of the liberation of man" in 2Bia. This statement can be interpreted as a defense of God because the global community is considered to be a child with God the Father patiently waiting for His creation to grow up into maturity by putting heavenly ideals into the foundation of all activity on earth.   Thus, Gutierrez wants the global population to take full responsibility for the way social structures operate, and in doing so he defends God against being responsible for corrupt governments.

Gutierrez draws on the authority of the Catholic Church in 2Bii to give him further justifications for humanity taking charge of creating social structures.   The Catholic Church allows their Church tradition to be authoritative along with special proclamations of the Pope. This is a very straightforward thing for a Catholic priest to do, and it is accepted as authoritative by Catholic believers. With the majority of Latin America being Catholic, this use of the Church's authority to persuade the vast populations of Catholic believers is very strong.   Gutierrez uses the message of Pope John XXIII, various Catholic manuscripts, and the Biblical theme of Jesus Christ being a liberator, to marshall evidence to support a social structural revolution. The persuasive power of these arguments in a largely Catholic population is very powerful. Thus, Gutierrez wisely uses sound audience analysis to arrange his arguments for humanity, specifically the Christian population in Latin America, to change the oppressive economic, social, and political structures operating within Latin America. Many Catholic priests have been murdered for proclaiming the themes of liberation theology. Without the notion of centers of power being challenged it would seem strange that people are being killed for proclaiming a message of change based on "loving your neighbor as yourself."

Indeed, Gutierrez calls for a social system based on "loving your neighbor as yourself" in 2Biib. Putting this idea in practice has thrust the church into the middle of the political arena in many countries, and many Christian groups have taken bold action in order to implement this ideal. For example, a group of Protestant Christians in Ecuador repossessed land that was not being used for the benefit of the local people. In the mind of these Christians the land belongs to God, and owners are at best only stewards of it. If the owners refuse to share their land with the people, then they are not being faithful stewards of it. Starr Bowen reports on how this policy works in practice.

> And if the farmer [owner] was not sharing his land with people, if he had more land than he needed while many people had nothing, then he wasn't keeping his land for God, ... the church ought to help get the land for the people who do need it.[25]

This activity allowed these Christians to invade local farmland and set up communal societies. In Ecuador, "[l]and invasion has become so commonplace that it is an accepted means of urban growth."[26] The basic motive for these groups is simple survival. Yet the communal nature of looking out for all of the society members is a liberation theology theme that puts the second greatest commandment of Jesus into concrete practice. Yet, this activity is not without cost as the following example of Chile indicates.

The attempt by Salvador Allende to implement socialism in Chile revealed the "internal and foreign opposition"[27] that waged war against this attempt. Allende combined policies that would put the majority of Chileans in control of all the foreign investments with a policy that would distribute the wealth to a broader base of people. Yet, the most crucial element in Allende's government was its democratic based socialism. Allende's aim was a socialistic democracy that put the majority of people in control of how the wealth of the nation was to be spent. The United States reportedly supported a military overthrow of Allende's government under the guise of protecting freedom and democracy, and they successfully negated the opportunity for establishing a democratic socialistic government. This was a big blow to liberation theologians because democratic socialism is one of their big ideals.

Yet beneath the overthrow of Allende's Chilean government lay the interest of preserving economic interests of multinational corporations (MNC's) which are based in the United States. In order to protect the investment interests of these MNC's the elite in Chile, along with increased military support of the United States, prevailed in overthrowing a newly formed government. The problem with Allende was that his policies did not fit the existing global interests of investors who controlled Chile's economy.[28] Without going into the explicit details of Allende's overthrow in Chile, this brief example gives us a good clue concerning what liberation theologians are facing with their preference for socialism.

Chile was the ideal nation for liberation theologians to focus on because Allende attempted to implement most of the basic economic reforms that liberation theologians seek. For example, democratic socialism empowered the people with a voice to control how the wealth of Chile was spent. The idea is that if the land is managed well, then everyone will have enough food and basic living necessities to subsist. Socialism is considered the only system that ensures basic equality for everyone. And putting the majority of people in control is considered to be the only way that the wealth of the nation will get evenly distributed.

Considering Allende's defeat in Chile allows us to view liberation theology intertextually, that is how it exists along side of other texts in the immediate context of its proclamation. As you recall, Gutierrez was heavily involved with the decision for the Christians to support Allende's democratic socialism. Yet, the liberation elements in Allende's decision to create a democratic socialism caused a drastic reaction from the United States and other countries who had large investments at stake in that nation. Quite simply, democratic socialism was going to shift the power of the financial assets from multinationals and international banks to the people of Chile. Protesters said the United States used one of the standard civil religion props -- namely, "freedom and democracy" -- to back a military overthrow of Allende. They said the U.S. rationale for this action was simple: Maintaining a working relationship with foreign governments that insures financial and political stability was considered more important than supporting systems that claim to exalt human equality. Yet, instead of giving up in the face of almost sure defeat, liberation theologians have taken concrete steps to overcome attempts of developed nations to maintain compatible Latin American governments. Nations like the United States are very significant texts, who demonstrate their significance when liberation theology themes are implemented by Third World governments like Chile. Yet as socialism continues to fail world-wide it will be very difficult for liberation theology to become a legitimate option.

In conclusion, Gutierrez rejects developmentalism because it hasn't worked in the past. Moreover, it is based on a developed center that keeps the Third World in a periphery position, which takes away the power of voice from Latin American people. Gutierrez does not promise that a government empowered by the majority would be any more liberating than the current systems. Yet Gutierrez wants the Latin American masses to take charge in creating a more just society. This in essence secularizes the kingdom-of-God, and can be interpreted as defending God from being held responsible for the corruption of governmental systems. Gutierrez draws on the office of the Pope, official documents of the Catholic Church, and the Biblical account of the liberation ministry of Jesus Christ to persuade his audience to accept his strategy of global liberation. Some Ecuadorian peasants have repossessed land after implementing liberation themes in their lived-experience. And the United States backed military coup of Allende's reign in Chile demonstrates how texts react to liberation theology themes when they become public practice.

The next proposition details the diachronic Christian response towards the relationship of spiritual salvation and the historical processes of man.

PROPOSITION THREE: There are different Christian responses to the notion of Christian spiritual salvation and the historical process of the liberation of man.

   A. Response: The New Christendom allows the believer to be responsible in the public arena, thus the ability to act politically, based on the teachings of St. Thomas Aquinas.

      i. Sanctioned Activity: To be a Christian is to accept and live in solidarity, faith, hope, and charity with mankind toward total communion.

      ii. Reason: The world and the Church are intimately connected and unable to be separated.

   B. Response: The plan for the Kingdom of God has no room for a profane, historical plan.

i. Sanctioned Activity: All participation in the world is done for the immediate benefit of the Church, based on Augustinian theology.

ii. Reason: The Church is to evangelize people and inspire the temporal order. The Priests are to give themselves only to this activity, and not participate in political action. Laymen are supposed to build up the Church and the world, but they are not to touch the autonomy of the temporal order to change it radically.

a. Result: These ideas result in hindering pastoral action, and in frustrating the lay ministry. Both situations are due to the growing awareness of an alienating situation.

ANALYSIS OF PROPOSITION THREE

In 3A Gutierrez sets up a dialectic of two responses. One response calls the church into the political arena, the other calls the church into aesthetic spiritual activity alone. The first response calls the church into the political arena, and this is a major theme of liberation theology. Calling the church into the political activism in Latin America is a very radical move. It is radical because the majority of the people who live in these Third World nations do not enjoy the basics of food, shelter, medical care, educational opportunity, and voting privileges that most United States citizens do. In the United States the poor are a minority with the majority being middle class. Thus, a call for the church to become politically active in the United States does not carry the same radical tone that it does in Latin America.

Thus, liberation theology does not affect U.S. Christians in the same way. Yet, Frederick Herzog offers three challenges to American Protestants issuing from Latin American liberation theology, namely: 1. The context for U.S. theology is the Black-White confrontation, not the Third World; 2. The ethical issue for theology is socialism vs. capitalism, not utopianism vs. realism; 3. The new hermeneutical challenge for theology is doing it by praxis and not with new theories.[29] Herzog adapted liberation themes to fit a U.S. audience that is predominately affluent. So instead of facing the issue of massive poverty as Latin

American theologians do, Herzog targets negative racial attitudes for liberation. He also wants a serious dialogue to be established on the ethical nature of capitalism vs. socialism in such a way that ranks these systems according the kind of humanism they produce. In this way Herzog calls U.S. Christians into the political arena, and the third point, which calls for theology based on praxis, gives the kind of radical hermeneutic needed to create substantial social changes within the existing U.S. system.

The United States as a text is radically different in orientation due to vastly different experiences. A simple critique of how the average U.S. citizens experiences the abundance of fundamental living necessities such as food, clothing, housing, medical care, educational opportunities, and job flexibility demonstrates how consciousness is partially formed by the material surroundings. The U.S. as a text does not relate to the text of Latin America where liberation theology originated. Thus, any empathetic understanding of the real situation of Latin America would require a prolonged exposure to the Latin American lived-experience.

In order to try to eliminate this consciousness-gap between these two texts, many meetings have been held in the United States on liberation theology with participants from the Latin American countries. This happened in the Detroit Conference of 1975. At this meeting many Latin American Christians shared information about their struggles for establishing a humane society in the midst of poverty and government corruption. In part the liberation theology meetings such as the one held at Detroit are opportunities for Latin American Christians to de-mythologize the strong civil religion that is so prevalent in the United States.

They talk about how difficult it is for the average U.S. citizen to believe the reports of criminal activity by the C.I.A. in foreign countries where it operates under the guise of protecting freedom and democracy. The difficultly most U.S. citizens have in realizing that for public officials to be elected into high public offices such as state governors, senators, congressmen, and even the national presidency, one must elicit the support of individuals who insist on being granted certain concessions for their support. Their de-mythologizing continues by contrasting a civil religion that states "In God We Trust" with a government based on money and military power operating under the guise of democracy. Latin American theologians give first-hand accounts of how the U.S. government hinder their efforts to create a more human form of government such as in the case of Allende's government in Chile. Of course the U.S. government believes it is stopping nightmares from manifesting when it shuts down Marxist backed governments. Thus, Latin American theologians suffer in their attempts to help U.S. Christians understand their situation because

Americans are far removed from being able to verify their accounts. The Vatican also hinders their voice.

Pope John Paul II is another major participant, or text, in the arena of liberation theology. Many of his statements concerning liberation theology are negative, especially concerning Marxist class-analysis and revolutionary class-struggle. Yet, some people defend the Pope from charges that he seeks only to maintain the status quo. For example, Gregory Baum says that John Paul II is very contemporary, and is decisively left in his orientation. Baum analyzes two documents written by John Paul II to prove this claim. In the first document Redemptor Hominis (1979), John Paul II says that Jesus' incarnation identifies God as being in solidarity with humanity, "therefore the dignity of people is grounded in Christ's presence to them."[30] And that the Catholic Church's mission is unified in proclaiming "the Gospel and the engagement on behalf of social justice."[31]

In the second document Laborem Exercens, John Paul II gives a radical notion that gives priority to "labor over power," and that the cause of human degradation is "domination built into the economic system."[32] In essence, John Paul II is giving credence to Marx's notion that the material realm controls aspects of human consciousness, "[b]ecause humans constitute themselves by laboring."[33] Yet John Paul II indicates that the worker's struggle is against the injustice of capital over labor, not against the ruling class. Thus, instead of a class-struggle, John Paul II urges the workers to participate in the decision-making processes of their labor as co-owners. John Paul II also recommends that representatives of all classes participate in the decisions of the governmental systems. This mixture of worker co-owners and participants along with class representation in government will protect "personal freedom and pluralism."[34]

The Pope has a very strong voice in the U.S., and his denunciation of Marxian class-analysis is very welcomed here. Yet, the Pope's anti-Marxist policy is considered to be a strong hinderance in the minds of liberation theologians, who use the Marxist critique of class-struggle to analyze the situation of rich vs. poor in Latin America. Proposition Four will detail liberation theologian's use of Marxism, and the strong anti-Marxist criticisms of those who disagree with its use. The point here is to note that the Pope is seen as a "reformist" because he does not support a radical change in structure as the liberation theologians do. John Paul II is most definitely a reformist, as Baum clearly documents his position of social justice within existing class stratifications in society, because he doesn't believe that the elimination of social class will solve the problems in Latin America. Yet, the Pope definitely supports the activity of the

Catholic Church seeking social justice, an activity that previous Vatican leaders have rejected.

A prime example of response 3B is contained in Pope Pius X (1903) statement: "Human society as established by God is made up of unequal elements. ... Accordingly it is in conformity with the order of human society as established by God that there be rulers and ruled, employers and employees, learned and ignorant, nobles and plebeians."[35] This attitude has prevailed in most of Christendom since the Apostle Paul instructed Christians that:

> Everyone must obey state authorities, because no authority exists without God's permission, and the existing authorities have been put there by God. Whoever opposes the existing authority opposes what God has ordered; and anyone who does so will bring judgment on himself. For rulers are not to be feared by those who do good, but by those who do evil. Would you like to be unafraid of the man in authority? Then do what is good, and he will praise you, because he is God's servant working for your own good. But if you do evil, then be afraid of him, because his power to punish is real. He is God's servant and carries out God's punishment on those who do evil. For this reason you must obey the authorities -- not just because of God's punishment, but also as a matter of conscience.
>
> That is why you pay taxes, because the authorities are working for God when they fulfill their duties. Pay, then, what you owe them; pay them your personal and property taxes, and show respect and honor for them all.[36] (Romans 13:1-7)

This passage directly concerns the principle issues in liberation theology. Pope Pius X basically outlined and sanctioned the inequality of social relationships within the Romans 13 passage above. Yet he forgot to mention the negative aspect of this passage. What if the ruling authorities were corrupt and had no concern for justice, or for doing anything except keeping their power with military and economic alliances? Are Christians supposed to submit to this type of government? The answer is mixed, the Christian right mainly submits to the government, and the Christian left mainly seeks to radically change it.

The response of 3B embodies the attitude of the Catholic Right. Carolyn Cook Dipboye traced the political struggle for human rights in Latin America from 1968 to 1980.[37] From Dipboye's we can understand the embeddedness of the Catholic right with the power structures of Latin America, and the Church's attempts to stop any efforts for liberation outside of existing structures. The following quote depicts this scenario.

> Operating to protect the self-interests of an economic and political elite, the governments, dubbing themselves "Christian" and the enemy "atheistically communist," anticipated extensive collaboration with the Church. They offered the Church such privileges as the teaching of religion in the public schools, the censorship of publications contrary to Christian sensitivities, the use of traditional Christian language in official state documents, the participation of government authorities and members of the armed forces in public acts of worship, and the subsidization of church institutions. The states would gain access to the masses through Christian traditions while the Church would gain prestige - a situation supposedly beneficial to both church and state.[38]

This quote sums up the Christian right's embeddedness with the established governments of Latin America, and the very strong dialectic against any group that refuses to operate within established structures.

The 1968 Medellin conference in Columbia targeted this embeddedness, and called the Catholic Church to renounce its ties with the governments of Latin America. They made this demand due to the oppressive effects of the economic structures on large populations of Catholic people all over Latin America. The relationship of the Catholic Church and Latin American governments revealed the Church's adherence to the government's "coercive violence."[39] This kind of violence can be understood from Dipboye's quote in the preceding paragraph. "Coercive violence" is usually described in non-violent terms because it never results in anyone being killed. Yet it is violence in the sense of prohibiting the freedoms of people who decide to work against the existing order. For example, the status quo controls the jobs in most Latin American countries so the power to withhold jobs determines the way people are able to survive. "Violence" is perpetuated by forcing those who oppose the status quo governments into a work-to-survive situation.

The Catholic Church began to renounce violations of human rights after the Medellin conference, and it "became the object of the state's disfavor."[40] By publically rebuking governmental injustice, the Catholic right openly intervened into the political realm. Thus the Vatican, which is predominately on the side of the political right, has now officially entered into the public arena with human rights issues. The distinguishing mark of the Catholic right now is the denunciation of Marxist class-analysis, and violent revolutionary class-struggle. In essence, Pope John Paul II supports the notion of working for social justice, but he refuses to accept Marx's class analysis. And in 1991 he seemed to support the notion that democratic capitalism is most in line with nature of God's human design in the encyclical Centesimus Annus. Thus, the Pope is clearly opposed to the radical Catholic left at this point.

From the Latin American governments point of view, the 3B response contains their ideal church attitude. Since liberation theologians have called the Catholic Church into the political sphere with the public denunciations of human rights violations, the Latin American governments have taken direct measures to protect their power and influence. For example, "the National Association for Private Enterprize (ANEP) and the growers' organization (FARO) joined forces" to support El Salvador's president Carlos Romero, who in turn "opposed land reform and promised to put the national clergy in order" and "clean the country of foreign revolutionary priests.""[41] And Brazil's "Tradition, Family, and Property (TFP) Society"[42] maintains strong ties with the government of Brazil. So, within the Catholic right there exists ultra right groups such as the TFP, and the more liberal right represented by figures such as Pope John Paul II.

In conclusion, there are two distinct solutions offered by the Christian community regarding the political nature of the church. One solution suggests isolation, and the other solution exhorts the Latin American church into political activity, which is very radical because of the poverty context that exists there, which most U.S. citizens cannot understand. Herzog attempts to re-contextualize liberation theology for the U.S. by targeting the racial black vs. white situation, by examining the ethics of economic systems, and by doing theology with a praxis hermeneutic. Liberation theologians try to eliminate the consciousness-gap with meetings in the U.S., but it is difficult for most U.S. Christians to realize either the covert international activity of the U.S. government, or the coercive violence of Latin American governments, who are embedded with the Catholic right. Pope John Paul II is viewed as a hinderance to liberation by many Latin American liberation theologians due to his rejection of Marxian class-analysis and his support of democratic capitalism, yet John Paul II is still considered a progressive within the Catholic right.

In proposition four Gutierrez identifies the specific strategies he proposes liberation theologians to take in attempting to change the economic, social, political, and religious structures in Latin America. Let us now examine it.

PROPOSITION FOUR. An Analysis of the situation of economic

dependence in Latin America will lead one to attempt to escape from it.

A. Reason: It didn't solve the prevailing economic system of poverty since it was implemented in the 1950s due to being structured on a developed model of the 1st world, rather than being structured on a underdeveloped Latin American model.

B. Reason: The dynamics of the capitalist economy lead to the establishment of a center and a periphery, which simultaneously generates progress and growing wealth for the few, but it generates social imbalances, political tensions, and poverty for the many.

   i. Activity: Multinational corporations must defend the status quo in order to stay in power, and must expand into underdeveloped areas with their system in order to make further profits.

C. Solution: Study the problem from the point of view of the dominated countries.

   i. Result: The perception that the poor dominated nations keep falling behind, which means the gap continues to grow between the rich and the poor.

   ii. Result: Observing a marked separation of two human groups, dominated and dominate, i.e. a class analysis.

   iii. Result: Latin American people will not emerge from their present status except by means of a profound transformation. A social revolution which will radically and qualitatively change the conditions in which they now live.

      a. Activity: Target the whole continent for a revolutionary process to begin as there is little chance for success for attempts limited to a national scope.

      b. Activity: Due to the defence of the status quo, many have sought to work outside of existing institutions and legal norms, sometimes even using violent political activity, including written statements reflecting on social revolution, direct intervention in worker's strikes, participation in public demonstrations, condemning unfair wages, exploitation, and starvation tactics.

c. Activity: Work to establish a democratic socialistic form of government with the social ownership of the means of production.

d. Activity: Using critical awareness, make the mass of poor people aware of their situation. Make them conscious of oppression, and urge them to commit themselves to the process of liberation along with other groups who are doing the same thing.

e. Activity: Equate working for the social revolution as being equal to working for the Kingdom of God, which requires a redefinition of the meaning of the faith.

f. Activity: Priests are to participate more actively in the pastoral decisions of the Church, and in calling the church to break its ties with an unjust order and stand with the oppressed, thus being in solidarity with the poor, and to work in secular jobs, or be supported in ways other than by taking support from the church.

g. Activity: Active participation of the oppressed so they can control their own destiny with the development of grass-roots organizations.

h. Activity: The church is to become an institution of social criticism.

ANALYSIS OF PROPOSITION FOUR

Proposition four gives us the specific details of Gutierrez's analysis of the situation, and his strategies for solving Latin American problems with liberation theology ideals. Notice how the most predominate theme in proposition four deals with economics questions. This is a result of the assimilation of Marxism with Christianity. Recall that Marx claimed that the material aspects of life governed the consciousness of the people, which means that changing the material conditions would change people's consciousness. Gutierrez has analyzed the Latin American situation by using Marxist materialistic terms. In proposition five Gutierrez will give the spiritual reasons for adopting Marx's materialistic analysis, but here he is mainly concerned with the material aspects.

A concrete example of 4A that justifies Gutierrez's rejection of any type of economic dependence was President Kennedy's attempt to implement an Alliance for Progress in 1961. Kennedy viewed Castro's revolution as a threat of losing Latin America to socialistic revolution. So Kennedy tried to implement a program that would raise the standard of living for people in Latin America, but he failed to understand that "the traditional oligarchy had no intentions of freely volunteering to give away or sell its lands, to tax itself more heavily, or to share power with a broader base of the population."[43] In essence the Alliance for Progress attempted to work within the current economic structures of Latin America in order to eliminate poverty. Kennedy naively assumed that those in power were going to be willing to share their wealth with the people. As a result, the corruption within the governments of Latin America consumed all of the benefits of the Alliance for Progress program. Yet, the embeddedness of multinationals within Latin American economic structures also aided in this failure.

Penny Lernoux demonstrates the inter-networking of corrupt government officials with multinational corporations by tracing the business activities of the Somoza family, who were the leaders before the 1979 Sandinesta revolution in Nicaragua. She documents that the Somoza family owned 5 million acres, and twenty-six of the biggest companies in Nicaragua. Peasants who were disregarded and banished into unwanted lands suffered from development attempts because when their land was developed Somoza made sure he acquired the newly valued land. For example, after a highway project connected the Northern Zelaya province, which was inhabited by a large Indian population, with the main southern provinces Somoza used his National Guard to purge the area in order to acquire this newly valued land. The following eyewitness account of this purging follows.

... in February 1976 five National Guard patrols stormed the [Zelaya] district. "They had a list of names," said an eyewitness, "and they moved from one isolated hut to the next, taking the men out, beating and torturing them in front of their families, demanding that they divulge the names of guerrilla collaborators in the area. These men were then marched out into the fields and shot." Women and children were also murdered, among them an eight-year-old boy who was hanged and then decapitated.[44]

The National Guard purged this area under the excuse of combating revolutionary guerrillas. At the end of this purge the land became the property of the chief of the National Guard in Zelaya, Commander Gonzalo Evertz. The above account demonstrates how money and greed for expansion governs the ethics of corrupt Latin American governments like the former Somoza regime. Nathaniel Davis, a former U.S. ambassador to Guatemala, says: "Money isn't everything. Love is the other 2 percent. I think this characterizes the United States' relationship with Latin America."[45] Thus, the multinationals, and the banking community of this country, are deeply embedded in the Latin American context, and this situation frustrates all efforts to eliminate poverty in these regions. Also, the vast gap between the rich and the poor have contributed to Gutierrez's adoption of Marx's notion of "class struggle."

The words "dominated" and "dominate" in 4Cii point to a class struggle. Indeed, Gutierrez borrows Marx's notion of class struggle in his analysis of the problems creating poverty in Latin America. In doing so he opens himself up to a host of criticism from people who regard as evil anything that has a hint of Marxism. Robert McAffee Brown defends Gutierrez by saying that Marx didn't invent the notion of class struggle, he simply reported that it existed.

> What actually happens with Gutierrez and with others close to him is something like this: they turn to the social sciences for help in understanding the dynamics of the world in which they live; among those they read is Marx, who describes a world in which a "class struggle" is going on. They look at Latin America ... and see that what Marx described is actually taking place: there is a "class struggle" going on, and it is being waged between the tiny "class" of the extremely wealthy and powerful. Marx, they discover, did not invent "class struggle;" he merely reported that it was taking place. The struggle would be there even if Marx had never appeared on the scene.[46]

In a later publication entitled We Drink from Our Own Wells, Gutierrez avoids all references to Marx as he felt that by using the Bible he didn't need Marx's analysis in order to draw the same conclusions about social injustice in Latin America. Specifically, Gutierrez used nearly 400 New Testament references to make the same observations.[47] Thus, even though the words "class struggle" is a non-Biblical theme, Gutierrez justified this notion by drawing on Biblical parallels. Thus, class struggle is seen as the most objective term of analysis for the current situation of dependence in Latin America.

> ... only a class-based analysis will enable us to see what is really involved in the opposition between oppressed countries on the one hand and dominant peoples on the other.[48]

And the action of establishing a socialistic form of government, along with the social ownership of the means of production, is deemed the best strategy for breaking the cycle of dependence.

Yet Gutierrez may have entangled himself by trying to justify a class struggle from a Biblical standpoint. His basic stance is that "class struggle is a fact and neutrality in this matter is impossible."[49] Michael Novak says that there is no valid proof that the Marxist notion of class struggle will prevail in gaining a new humanity. His comparison of medical care, education, and quality of life between socialist countries and capitalist countries show that the capitalist countries are better off in every category.

> [T]he greatest chances for improving the concrete daily life of human beings everywhere lie not with the forces of Marxist "liberation" but with the forces of democratic capitalism.[50]

Thus Novak believes that democratic capitalism will produce a better quality of life for the global community. Yet Gutierrez counters Novak's position by analyzing the modern age from the perspective of both the powerful and the powerless.

Gutierrez gives a critique of domination according to the experience of the dominant and the dominated over a period of time. Our second phenomenology tool allows us to enter into this lived-world where people's consciousness have been formed by the prevailing economic and political systems that have existed in previous generations. From the point of view of the dominant class the modern age of the sixteenth century exalted human reason, and "[r]ational questioning, observation, and empirical proof replaced dogmatic assertion[s] and deduction from First Principles."[51] The church at this time rejected this shift from theology to human reason.

> The modern age and premodern Christianity were natural antagonists. One Truth precluded religious tolerance; dogma was inimical to science; Divine Providence was clearly inimical to

individual autonomy, liberty, and initiative, and hence profoundly immoral. Intelligent and subtle people resolved this painful schism in various ways: Some kept intellectual freedom and belief in a personal God in separate mental compartments; atheists denied God's existence; eighteenth-century Deists tried to formulate a rational religion, free of dogma and authoritarianism and hence universally acceptable to enlightened minds but also completely tolerant of dissent -- religion for an intellectual elite.[52]

The modern age rejected religious dogma, and in doing so put religion in the category of being redundant for the oncoming scientific world. This situation formed the consciousness of those in power in such a way that it allowed most people to continue in the path of industrialization without any concern for Christianity's mandate to "love others as we love ourselves." Operating within a capitalistic structure, the modern age provided power and wealth to those who followed its path. Thus, the closed mind of the church during the modern age gave many individuals the liberty to ignore the moral and ethical teachings of the church, and this situation became the source of oppression during the industrial expansion of developing countries.

We can view the oppressive manifestations of this situation by switching perspectives from the dominant to the dominated in order to determine how the dominated viewed the progress of the modern age. Gutierrez, who describes himself as an individual living in a dominated country, portrays the modern age expansion into Latin America as resulting in oppression for the entire region.

> In Western Europe the modern process engendered political freedom and individual liberty. Elsewhere that same process meant new and more refined forms of exploitation of the common people.[53]

In essence, the modern age capitalistic expansion into Latin America is viewed by Gutierrez as cultural, social, economic, religious, and political enslavement by those who gained power by expanding business operations internationally. He feels that ethnocentric European cultural and social ideals were imposed on the non-Western societies of Latin America. The consequences were economic and political enslavement which permitted only political decisions that favored the economic establishment of Western Europe's expansionism. Another consequence was religious enslavement in the imposition of Catholicism upon native religious structures in such a way that the later were given no real alternative in choosing their religion.

Thus, Gutierrez views the experience of the modern age as being massively oppressive to Latin America.

As a result of liberation theologians like Gutierrez, who re-writes history from the dominated perspective, and through the conscientization projects of liberation theologians with the masses of poverty stricken people, many Latin American Christians are combining modern age scientific analysis with Biblical morality for the purpose of liberating themselves from the entrenched dependence of developed countries as the following quote by Gutierrez indicates.

The Latin American poor seek to eradicate their misery, not ameliorate it; hence they choose social revolution rather than reform, liberation rather than development, and socialism rather than liberalization.[54]

The Latin American people have analyzed their situation using the methods of the social sciences, and they are plotting long range strategies in order to eliminate the oppressive situations in which they live. Thus, the mixture of the modern age with Biblical morality.

In 4Ciii Gutierrez calls for a radical revolution. After Enrique Dussel traced the global domination patterns of center and periphery, he said that the only major country liberated from economic domination was China.[55] China is viewed as being set free from the domination patterns of the modern age. And in 4Ciiia Gutierrez wants Latin America to gain this type of deliverance with a total continental deliverance from dominating foreign policies. The decision for total continental liberation was made after considering Allende's plight in Chile, which graphically demonstrated how small countries can be reduced to shambles when they try to buck the international economic system. Thus, liberation theologians target the entire continent of Latin America for radical change as the following quote by a group of liberation theologians in Chicago demonstrates. As "genuine liberation demands participation in the international struggle against class exploitation, racism, sexism, and imperialism."[56]

Yet, many have concluded that Latin America doesn't have anything near the capitalistic structures they so adamantly reject. For example, Dr. Paul Morgan and Dr. Edd Noell, professors of economics and business at Westmont College in Santa Barbara, California, say that Latin America has an economy based on an earlier model of "European mercantilism" that flourished in Europe from "1500 to 1800."[57] This system is noted for giving power to the state by limiting competition through extensive regulation thus thwarting enterprize and incentive, and by being completely corrupted by graft, bribe, and protectionism. Thus, Morgan and Noell have labeled the economic system of Latin American as a "state capitalism" as opposed to a "market capitalism." They believe that an economic system based on market capitalism would "liberate" the poor of Latin America based on a historical analysis of its past performance from other countries who have adopted it.[58] Thus Gutierrez is charged with not understanding the economic system he rejects, and opting to use a socialistic system that has no historical precedent for liberating anyone.

In 4Ciiib Gutierrez mentions violence as an activity Christians should take in order to gain liberation if it is necessary. He does not directly refer to killing people in guerilla revolutionary warfare. But, all previous examples of class struggle in previous revolutionary activity in Latin American clearly advocates this strategy. Violent class struggle is the focal point of most public rebukes from the Vatican. The Vatican clearly states that "systematic recourse to violence put forward as the necessary path to liberation has to be condemned as a destructive illusion and one that opens the way to new forms of servitude."[59] This warning is issued in the context of Nicaragua's revolution where many liberation theologians took up weapons and helped fight in the revolution. "Paul Schmitz, a U.S. priest who is now a bishop in Nicaragua, declared that the country [Nicaragua] is a laboratory for all of Latin America."[60] The theology of violence, used by some liberation theologians, is summed up with the following quote:

> The mystery of the cross is deeper than any one interpretation, but it would be a distortion to take it as a sign of servility, indifference, or cringing in the face of tyrannic power. Perhaps active non-violent struggle against injustice is the method most desired by Christians but the decision to participate in armed struggle may often be the only option open. This brings to mind Luther's concept of 'the strange works of love.'[61]

L. Michael Jendrzejczyk, a liberation theologian who advocates the possible use of violence, wants to set the limits of violence by having a parallel system to the governments use of it.[62] In other words, Jendrzejczyk wants to allow the opposition to set the limits on violence. In reality this means is that there will be no limits on violence. But, Jose Miguez Bonino says that violence should be considered on the basis of the human cost involved of the liberators and the enemy.[63] Bonino also says that "superficial sentimentalism" such as "reconciliation, pardon or peace," are "equivocating, reactionary attitudes ... [that] in the long run [are] more costly in human life and suffering and less respectful of the person."[64] Thus, Bonino wants the criteria of legitimate violence to be determined by analyzing "how it is possible to humanize this struggle [of human oppression] in the greatest possible degree."[65] Yet this approach to the notion of violence still draws public rebukes from the Vatican because it still leaves the possibility open for a revolutionary class struggle, which predictably includes widespread loss of life. But, liberation theologians are angered by these rebukes from the Pope and North American Christians.

Latin American liberation theologians are distressed by North American theologians, who they say are enjoying the fruits of liberation from British domination and who piously denounce the use of violence to change society. Christians who use the historical account of Jesus' ministry, which focused on transformation of individuals rather than transforming prevailing social structures, to negate Christian political activity are countered by liberation theologians who say that Jesus would be a part of social transformation if He were walking the earth today. Liberation theologians say that we "can speculate 'had social conditions been transformable in the first century in a way similar to what is now possible through appropriate technological and socioeconomic policies, Jesus would most likely have demanded such a transformation and acted to bring it about.'"[66] The opinions on the issue of violence among liberation theologians are still very diverse as we discussed more fully in Chapter Two, but the desire for democratic socialism is nearly unanimous.

In 4Ciiic Gutierrez wants a democratic socialistic form of government with the social ownership of the means of production. This desire is a sign pointing to his affirmation that people can "be transformed by altering socio-cultural structures."[67] As you recall, this notion is based in Marx's concept that the material factors of life are key ingredients in the formation of people's consciousness. Gutierrez doesn't hold to an absolute materialist position because he believes that individuals must undergo an inner change of attitude in order for social structure changes to work. Thus, he holds to an interdependence of attitude and social structure.

> The view that a structural transformation will automatically produce different human beings is no more and no less "mechanistic" than the view that a "personal change of heart" will automatically lead to a transformation of society. Any such mechanistic views are naive and unrealistic.[68]

Cuba supports this idea of material and spiritual interdependence as its new official position is that "Christians won't be free without socialism, and socialism won't be built on this continent [Latin America] without Christians."[69] This idea has already been stated in terms of the meshing of the scientific modern age with Biblical morality. In essence, democratic socialism is viewed as the best form of government, and in order for it to operate efficiently it needs the morality provided by Christianity. Thus, Gutierrez is trying to convince Latin American Christians to support radical democratic socialism. Of course not all agree with Gutierrez as Hernado de Soto "the most influential person in contemporary Latin America [makes] a persuasive case for capitalism in his best selling book The Other Path.[70]

Yet the Rev. Donald J. Keefe, S.J., an opponent of liberation theology, says that the Church must be renewed by repenting from not practicing the teachings of the church in public. Keefe says that:

only by refusing the isolation of the faith, by taking the truth of Christ ... into all the dimensions of public life. It is the failure to do this, on the right as well as on the left, that has established real injustice and oppression in the Christian world, and the only liberation from such social structures that is real is that which is dynamically present in the worship of the church. The reality of liberation is the reality of the new creation. There is no other, and all its counterfeits are finally idolatrous.[71]

Thus, Keefe challenges Gutierrez's notion by using a social gospel theme that implements Christian ideals in the existing society. In contrast, Gutierrez insists on uniting the masses of the poor in order to create a radical social structural revolution.

Liberation theologians would say that "a changed person in an unchanged system usually doesn't make much difference."[72] And in the U.S. "American civil religion calls us to honor and respect but never challenge ... [o]ur economic order [which] is dominated by large corporations whose growth and survival is fostered by stability."[73] Yet the very essence of American civil religion, such as the insignia of "In God We Trust" on U.S. currency, closely identifies with liberation themes. The U.S. war of independence from British domination is the type of struggle Latin American liberation theologians desire. The United States perpetuates a civil religion that has the same ideals as liberation theology. Indeed, liberation theologians are attempting to create a Latin American civil religion similar to the American model, as the following quote indicates.

the best strands of America's civil religion is a liberation theology and the Latin American liberation theology is an attempt to create a civil religion.[74]

Many say that the foreign policies of the U.S. violate the tenets of this civil religion by dominating the economic structure of the Third World as at times in God we trust, but in our own national economic and military interests we act. Liberation theologians like Gutierrez wants the poor to unite to overcome their present situation of dominance.

> The poor, the oppressed, must bring about a social appropriation of the gospel, and to do so they must seize it from the hands of the powerful of this world.[75]

Thus, liberation theologians seek liberation from the domination of the developed world.

Poverty is one of the main problems liberation theologians desire to solve. It is seen as more of a structural problem than a problem of individual sin.[76] Yet in post-revolutionary Cuba many Christians have trouble accepting the Marxist "materialist explanation of life."[77] The problem is that Christians hold to spirituality as being more important than the material structural arrangements. This notion of making a priority of the spiritual aspects over the material aspects of life is grounded in the New Testament passage where the Apostle Paul writes:

> ... I have learned to be satisfied with what I have. I know what it is to be in need and what it is to have more than enough. I have learned this secret, so that anywhere, at any time, I am content, whether I am full or hungry, whether I have too much or too little. I have the strength to face all conditions by the power that Christ gives me.[78] (Philippians 4:11b-13)

Gutierrez combines the material with the spiritual in order to by-pass this problem of a spirituality that does not consider material welfare. But, the Cuban Christian disillusionment with Marxist materialism results from living in a radically different context from the predominate Christian context Gutierrez has in Latin America. Cuban Christians were persecuted during the formative years of Castro's regime. Cuban Christians have only recently been allowed to openly practice Christianity. This is a very different situation for liberation theologians in Latin America because they want to start a revolution from a Catholic Christian base, which will allow the participants to maintain the spiritual base during the establishment of the new material society. Thus, the Cuban Christian disillusionment with Marxist materialism will not be a prevailing problem for liberation theologians. One of the reasons is that liberation theologians encourage the establishment of small intimate spiritual communities.

These communities are mentioned in 4Ciiig, and liberation theologians consider them to be the most important activities of liberation theology. Grass-roots organizations, or base Christian communities, are the major workers of liberation theology. These communities are called "grass-roots" and "base" because they usually consist of the lowest class of people within society.[79] Leonardo Boff characterizes these communities with five basic points. First of all, these communities are small cell groups of people who take responsibility for understanding and propagating their faith. Secondly, these cell groups bring real life problems to the Biblical texts to find answers and solutions to their problems. The third characteristic is that these groups form a community in which all the members are equal in the sense of sharing their faith, presiding over the sacraments, and using spiritual gifts for the purpose of serving the community. These gifts are called "charisms," which are grace gifts of service. The fourth point is that these groups analyze the problems they face, and then take social action to solve these problems. The fifth and last characteristic of these base Christian communities is that they celebrate the spiritual liberation gained in Jesus Christ.[80]

The simple message behind these communities is that "people who work and pray together can achieve a better life for themselves and their community."[81] The basic instruction among the Zelaya Christian communities in Nicaragua are: "love your neighbor, know your legal rights, and be proud of your Indian heritage."[82] Among preliterate groups these simple but powerful messages contain the necessary ingredients of practical liberation theology. Yet these base Christian communities are challenging the structures of the religious hierarchy. Boff charted these challenges as the following diagram indicates.[83]

REALITY

1. Clericalism: a Church of the priests.
2. Imposing Church anonymous, no questions, no information; institution, obedience to laws.
3. Alienation: Church is only rites and sacraments; allied with the rich.

GOAL

1. Church of the people not for the people but a Church with them.
2. Fraternity, dialogue, services; horizontal, relationships, co-responsibility.
3. Seeking out the poor an incarnated Church denounces injustices, defends the exploited, and is conscious of human rights.

REFLECTION

1. Church as People of God.
2. Church communion, community of faith and love; sacrament sign.
3. Prophetic Church, liberator, community of Abraham sacrament - instrument of liberation.

PRAXIS

1. Open dialogue, equality, listening to the people, participation. The priests change.
2. The people change, communicate and express themselves in the liturgy, undertaking services. Community not of obedience but of love.
3. Social commitment; groups for conscientization and reflection on human rights formation of base ecclesial community.

Boff goes on to argue for an alternative church structure in which "charism" is the organizing principle.[84] In other words, a church of the people is organized in such a way in which everyone participates by using their spiritual gifts in serving the believing community and society at large. Every person is assumed to have some type of spiritual gift that is to be implemented in the service of the believers and the community. For example, the ability to be an administrator, a carpenter, and a mechanic are considered manifestations of spiritual gifts, but they also include the ability to give wise council, pray for physical healing, etc. Thus, spiritual gifts are considered to be talents that individuals use to serve others. But, the structural changes of authority and voice within this transformation creates tension. Basically, tension results as the bishops and priests are at best only considered to be members of a community of believers, and the Pope's office becomes redundant because of his separation from the real life situation of Latin America. Tension also results from these grass-root communities because they are becoming a strong political voice.

By taking sides with the poor and helping them gain a political voice, liberation theologians proclaim their liberation from those who oppress them. An intertextual analysis of this activity enables us to interpret how this activity is assimilated by other texts such as the United States. The United States is fairly insulated from liberation theology because those in power have created an economic system that rewards the middle class, which is the largest social class in this country. The demands for social reform are not felt in the United States because many people are able to own their own home, provide medical care for their family, educate their children, and enjoy a broad range of freedoms such as job choice, geographical flexibility, etc. Surprisingly, The National Conference of Catholic Bishops in the United States supported the liberation theology activity of opting for the poor with a written document on November 13, 1986, which stated:

> The document advocates economic policies that guarantee a job with decent pay for all who can and will work, cooperation by government, business, labor and private agencies to do more for the poor, more equitable distribution of wealth, government policies that will give more help to troubled family-owned farms, and more U.S. concern for the poor in Third World nations and their economies. ... It also criticized the 300 billion annual U.S. military budget.[85]

If we raise our analysis up from the intertextual analysis of how the activity of opting for the poor has caught on among other countries to a metatextual analysis concerning why U.S. Catholics would take on this activity, we can interpret this activity in another way. For example, liberation theology literature is very extensive in the United States due to the publishing efforts of Orbis Books in Maryknoll, New York. Due to this exposure to liberation literature among U.S. Catholics, the decision to opt for the poor in the United States could easily be seen as simply a political move by a wise Catholic priest hierarchy. Interest in helping the poor could only be mentioned to lead the Catholic laity into believing that the church is concerned for the poor. Thus, this move can be suspected of being a political maneuver by those who want to say the right things in order to keep their power of voice.

Yet, the priests who have carried out the mandate of denouncing injustice in Latin America have met with violent resistance. "During the 1970s approximately 850 bishops, priests, and nuns were murdered, arrested, and/or tortured."[86]   The death of these martyrs is a sign that speaks for their sincere belief in the message of liberation they proclaim. The Catholic priests in the U.S. may play perceptual politics with the flock, but the Latin American priests put their lives in jeopardy when they decide to opt for the poor. Thus, the life threatening context of Latin America is a sign that purges any doubts about the sincere motivations of those who are willing to die for proclaiming themes of liberation. Thus, anyone who opts for the poor in Latin America is definitely sincere regardless whether their activity is right or wrong.

In conclusion, proposition four gives us the materialistic side of liberation theology along with the specific political strategies used to change the economic, social, political, and religious structures of Latin America. Basically, Gutierrez rejects any form of "aid" that perpetuates dependence because this type of revisionism has not worked in the past due to the embeddedness of Latin American economics within multinational corporations.   Marxist class analysis is considered the most scientific method to analyze the Latin American situation. Gutierrez gives foundation to his use of class analysis with a diachronic analysis of the effect of the modern age on Latin America. By critiquing modern age activity from both the view of the dominate and the dominated, he paints a picture of ruthless scientism stimulated by the need for industrial expansionism into Latin America in order to ensure power. From the view of the dominate this activity was a logical way to increase economic power, but from the view of Latin America this activity brought slavery in a host of ways.

Gutierrez offers a solution of mixing modern age scientism with Christian morality in order to create a new society based on democratic socialism. The question of revolutionary violence in order to establish this type of government is a controversial issue among liberation theologians. Some openly advocate violence, and others only allow its possibility. Yet the Vatican publically denounces all possibilities of violence as being equated with Christian morality. But the ideals of democratic socialism are almost completely accepted by liberation theologians.   And the base-Christian communities are the groups these theologians encourage in order to achieve this type of government. But these communities also challenge the traditional Catholic hierarchy because the laity are empowered with voice and authority within these communities.

Proposition five will now give the spiritual side of liberation theology.   In essence, the gospel message is shown to completely support the humanization that liberation theologians desire.

PROPOSITION FIVE: Salvation and liberation are intimately related.

A. Example: Salvation is the central theme of Christianity.

i. Qualification: It is cure for sin in this life; and in the next life, which means salvation is both earthly and heavenly oriented.   In essence, salvation is not something other-worldly, in regard to which the present life is merely a test. It is the communion of men with God and the communion of men among themselves, and it embraces all human reality, transforms it, and leads it to its fullness in Christ.

a. Specific: People are saved if they open themselves up to God and to others, even if they are not clearly aware they are doing so.   Spiritually, a person is converted to the other, and especially the oppressed person, the exploited social class, the despised race, and the dominated country.

ii. Qualification: Creation is a salvic act, which means it is the initiation of God's saving action in history, and history is unified under creation and salvation.

B. Example: God saves through liberation as in the Exodus account of the Old Testament, and this is a political liberation.

i. Qualification: Salvation is a re-creation towards a complete fulfillment, the freedom from misery and alienation.

C. Example: Eschatological promises, or the end time prophecies, are to be fulfilled here on earth.

i. Qualification: Establishing the kingdom of God on earth is an ongoing act that will eventually save the whole earth when it is fully established, thus the elimination of misery and exploitation will be a sign of the coming of the Kingdom.   In other words, the struggle for a just world in which there is no oppression, servitude, or alienated work will signify the coming of the Kingdom of God on earth.

ii. Result: A theology of hope emerges from these promises, which stresses liberation <u>will</u> occur on earth.

D. Example: Christ's death and resurrection redeems man from sin and all its consequences such as hunger, misery, oppression, ignorance, injustice, hatred, etc.

E. Example: When Christ became a man it indicates that the temple of God is humanity.

    i. Specific: Loving God means loving ones neighbor, and love is accomplished by doing justice. In essence, exploitation of the humble and poor worker is a sin towards God.

F. Example: The church's mission is to serve all people, in such a way that it is to be a visual sacrament that clearly demonstrates communion with God and the unity of all mankind.

    i. Specific: The Eucharist is a sign of human brotherhood in the sharing of God's gift of life.

        a. Result: Class divisions must cease.

        b. Result: Material poverty must be eliminated because it is a concrete sign that nullifies brotherhood. Spiritual poverty is an attitude of openness to God and spiritual childhood, and is thus not the focus of liberation.

        c. Result: Christian poverty, which is a voluntary poverty and an expression of love, is a decision of solidarity with the poor and it is a protest against poverty.

G. Example: Moses and the Old Testament prophets rejected poverty for any of God's people.

    i. Specific: People are created in the image of God, thus their God given responsibility is to rule over nature, not each other, (Gen.1:26, 2:15).

ANALYSIS OF PROPOSITION FIVE

As you recall, proposition four provided the materialistic foundation of liberation theology, and now proposition five gives the spiritual foundations for it. The three main features of the spiritual foundations of liberation theology are: (1) the kingdom of God becomes secularized; (2) the notion of salvation from sin is extended into all aspects of life such as in salvation from material poverty; and (3) the second greatest commandment to "love your neighbor as yourself" is extended into the total lived-experience. These three distinctive characteristics of liberation theology set this movement apart from other religious movements, and these notions are unique Latin American contributions to theology.

In 5Ai Gutierrez stresses the vertical relationship with God in salvation, and the horizontal relationship with men in liberation. Some have criticized liberation theology by saying it is only concerned with social justice and thus ignores the vertical emphasis of heavenly oriented theology. In 1983, Gutierrez countered this criticism with the notion that both the vertical and horizontal aspects of liberation theology are present in his book A Theology of Liberation, and 5Ai in the propositional outline above clearly validates his claim.[87] Gutierrez holds to a total communion of humanity, which points to the melting of racial and gender barriers.

Indeed, the communion mentioned in 5Ai points to racial and gender liberation with the idea of human communion with God and with each other. Racial and gender liberation groups have the common thread of interest with Latin American liberation theologians for a more human world. Racial liberation theologians want a society in which people are not marginalized because of their racial heritage. Speaking for the Blacks in the United States, James H. Cone says that "[l]iberation knows no color bar; the very nature of the gospel is universalism, i.e., a liberation that embraces the whole of humanity."[88] The basic message of racial liberation theology follows along the lines of Martin Luther King, who wanted a world in which skin color and ethnic heritage ceased to be barriers to global human communion. The exact opposite of these ideals is the ideology/theology of the Ku Klux Klan, a group which considers the white race as being endowed by God to rule over all other races. The KKK shares the same ideals with men who view women as being the weaker sex, thus unworthy of equal treatment.

Elizabeth Schussler Fiorenza, representing gender liberation, targets gender domination social structures as oppressive to the full development of women in Western society.

the new feminist movement radically criticizes the myth and structures of a society and culture which keeps women down. The women's liberation movement demands a restructuring of societal institutions and a redefinition of cultural images and roles of women and men, if women are to become autonomous human persons and achieve economic and political equality.[89]

Fiorenza uses a critical hermeneutic to analyze social structures to determine how one group has power at the expense of another. In this case, the patriarchal system of male leadership is found to be in power over the female population by an intricate attitudinal structure that marginalizes individuals on the basis of gender. In essence, gender liberationists want to change the attitudinal structures of society in order to gain gender equality.

In 5Aia Gutierrez clarifies the notion of salvation by saying that people are converted when they open themselves up to God and to others. This entails demonstrating communion with God by living in communion with one's neighbor. Gutierrez states that this can be accomplished even if the individual is not aware of this action. These ideas run counter to the conservative Protestant tradition of salvation, which maintains a strict interpretation of salvation from the New Testament. Basically, the New Testament says that people are saved when they accept Jesus Christ as their Savior and commit themselves to doing His will in their lives. Conversion is based on a conscious decision of faith in Christ, and in obeying His teachings. A person is saved, according to the New Testament, when the Holy Spirit lives in the believer, which signifies God's seal of acceptance. Thus, from this perspective liberation theology is clearly heretical, and many Bible believing Protestants rebuke Gutierrez on this issue. And, even Protestants and Catholics agree on denouncing Gutierrez for extending salvation into all aspects of life.

Indeed, the Protestant tradition agrees with the Pope's denunciation of salvation being equated with the social, economic, and political liberation. Gutierrez clearly combines salvation of sin with liberation from social, economic, and political structures that are used to oppress people. John Paul II says that it is a "mistake to state that political, economic, and social liberation coincide with salvation in Jesus Christ."[90]   And Protestants affirm this denunciation and say that Gutierrez equates salvation with "building the new society," and conversion with the "commitment to transforming human reality."[91]   New Testament theology clearly equates salvation with the individual being saved from sin, and not with changing oppressive social structures.[92]

Gutierrez's notion of salvation also differs from the Pope's conception of what an orthodox bishop is to teach. In his Puebla address to Latin American bishops John Paul II re-iterated that: "There is no authentic evangelization so long as one does not announce the name, the teaching, the life, the promises, the Kingdom, the mystery of Jesus of Nazareth, the Son of God."[93] John Paul II wants this message to be received by people, who will then in turn live out the Christian faith in the social context. In this way, the bishop's job is to teach the truth of the Gospel, and the people are to act on these teachings to transform the world.

In 5C and 5Ci-ii, liberation theology distinguishes itself from other Christian movements like the Anabaptists, who are a group of Christians who seclude themselves from the world by living in communal farm systems in the Amish tradition. The Anabaptists share liberation theology's concern for justice, love, and peace, but they differ significantly on the role of the church in secular society. Liberation theology calls for the church to become directly involved with the economic, political, social, and religious aspects of society.

The Anabaptists became involved in society during their gestation period in the sixteenth century and became severely oppressed by political opponents for their social criticisms. After this they decided that society could not be changed by people, and that they were not responsible for participating within it any longer.[94] Instead of participating with the world, the Anabaptists now create their own social network that matches their beliefs, and they live within these communities with very little outside contact. By contrast, liberation theologians have stressed the same type of activity in the formation of base-Christian communities, but these communities involve themselves in the affairs of society. Thus, liberation theologians and the Anabaptists share the concern for social justice, but they differ over the notion that the Kingdom of God can be established on earth. But there is a mixture of opinions in Latin America concerning the churches' involvement in secular society.

Raymond K. Dehainaut describes four ways the Latin American religious community has responded to the ideology of their social institutions: (1) Pentecostal fundamentalist Christians avoid any association with worldly politics; (2) Conservative Christians participate with political issues in order to maintain the status quo, with primary concern devoted to converting individuals into the Christian faith; (3) Ecumenical Christians, which mainly consist of Roman Catholic bishops, show concern for a "social and economic development;" (4) Revolutionary Christians advocate social reform, some advocate peaceful means while others advocate revolutionary violence,[95] but all revolutionary Christians agree to the following:

> ... that rapid and profound changes must be made in economic, social, and political structures. ... that the traditional ruling classes must be deposed and deprived of all special privileges. ... that Latin America must be freed from dependency on the United States and all other highly developed nations. ... They are critical of all "reformist" solutions.[96]

Liberation theologians identify with the Revolutionary Christians in theology and ideology, and use the Marxist class analysis in order to identify and then change the structures that create and maintain poverty.

Gutierrez identifies the Eucharist with the radical revolutionary Christians as the results listed under 5Fi revolve around eliminating class divisions and poverty. Poverty is considered to be a sinful situation created by selfish individuals operating within a manipulative framework of a capitalist economic structure. The Eucharist, or the Lord's Supper, is a powerful New Testament ideal that brings Christians together around the blood of Christ. Gutierrez wants humanity to embrace this activity in order to eliminate poverty, as one cannot take the Lord's Supper and continue to operate within structures that allow a distinction between rich and poor.

Indeed, taking sides with the poor is equated with taking God's side, and refusing to take sides with the poor is considered a rejection of God. Gutierrez draws on a number of Old Testament passages along with the ideals of the Eucharist in order to "Biblify" this notion as the passage found in the book of Amos demonstrates:

> Thus says the Lord, ... I will not revoke its [Israel's] punishment, Because they sell the righteous for money and the needy for a pair of sandals. These who pant after the very dust of the earth on the head of the helpless also turn aside the way of the humble.[97]

This emphasis upon the direct activity of Christians in the world is in sharp contrast with groups who hold to a separatist theology that instructs believers to avoid all worldly contact. Beatriz Melano Couch of Argentina starts with the idea of the church being active in the world, and then traces the diachronic development of this idea within his lifetime.

> We have seen appear in the course of more than twenty-five years different types of theological reflection and of ecclesiastical approaches to mission. We have seen it move in this direction:

from a call to a relevant or incarnate theology to a theology of development to an ecumenical theology to a theology of history to a theology of liberation.

... This process has in its background a philosophical counterpart that can be schematized as follows: liberal idealism (process of desacralization of society) to pragmatism (development interest) to utopian socialism.[98]

Thus, Couch has seen the evolution of the theology that posits the church becoming politically active in society, and liberation theology proclaims the pinnacle of this evolutionary process by calling Christians into political involvement.

In 5F, Gutierrez challenges the church to serve all people in a way that visually demonstrates communion with God and the global community. Leonardo Boff, a Brazilian priest and one of the most productive publishers of liberation theology, takes up this theme of calling the church into service and not power. Boff asks tough questions such as the following.

Is it true, Father Boff asks, that the church needs power, prudence, concessions, the typical tricks of pagan power, all criticized by Jesus (MT. 10:42), or does its strength lie precisely in weakness, the renunciation of all security, prophetic courage, as practiced by the church of the first three centuries?[99]

This type of questioning makes the traditional Catholic hierarchy uneasy as Boff calls into question the "hierarchy's present monopoly of institutional and corporate power to its custody of the Gospel, of theology and of the sacraments."[100] One can understand why Cardinal Joseph Ratzinger, an official Catholic theologian, would write a harsh critique of Boff's work.

The Vatican has long been concerned about Boff's 1981 book, Church: Charism & Power, and last September he was summoned to Rome for interrogation [by Ratzinger]. In a forceful March "notification," the Vatican rejected the book's Marxist-influenced examination of the Roman Catholic Church. Boff theorized about the sacraments as consumer products controlled by the bishops and priests. His ideas, said Rome, "endanger" the faith.[101]

In 1992 Boff left the Catholic Church because he said the Vatican "pressured me, prohibited me from teaching, speaking or writing and have punished me."[102] Anytime someone questions the Catholic Church's traditional power and authority structures significantly over time as Boff did, the Church hierarchy predictably fights back. Earlier Cardinal Ratzinger attempted to eliminate the voice of Gutierrez as well.

Ratzinger pursued Gutierrez with a year long investigation of his theology, which was conducted by the Peruvian clergy in 1983. When Peru's bishops came up with a split decision about Gutierrez and his liberation theology, "a majority report of censure and a minority report defending Gutierrez," Ratzinger aborted the investigation because "[he] apparently had hoped for a single unequivocal stance from the bishops which would not only discredit liberation theology in Peru but damage it throughout Latin America."[103] This brief episode gives the immediate sense of a massive power play among the Catholic hierarchy over the issue of liberation theology. When Gutierrez answered the question about how he unexpectedly evaded Ratzinger's investigation he responded: "You mean why, besides the work of the Spirit?"[104]

Yet we shouldn't be fooled into thinking Gutierrez is naive about power and how one obtains it as his liberation theology has struck at the foundation stones of the Catholic Church, which has made the Catholic hierarchy extremely defensive. But, instead of the ideological revolutionary who wants to replace one corrupt governmental system with another totalitarian regime, Gutierrez seeks to empower the masses of Latin America with a voice of their own, with adequate living conditions, with a hope in this life, and with the dignity he believes every human being deserves. In essence, Gutierrez has a very simple strategy that seeks to change the social, economic, political, and religious structures of the global community into following Jesus's "love-your-neighbor" mandate. Gutierrez believes that if any structural element is out of line with this policy, then it simply needs to be changed, so that authentic liberation will prevail. He tries to be very careful that the gospel message is not used as a smoke-screen to cover up injustice.

> the communication of the message reread from the standpoint of the other, of the poor and oppressed, will serve to unmask any attempt to ideologize the Gospel and justify a situation contrary to the most elemental demands of the Gospel.[105]

Thus, Gutierrez is on the alert to any ideology that uses the Christian faith for the purpose of maintaining power and control, and his strategies of liberation theology point to a very wise individual who makes the establishment nervous by exposing the inner networks of power structures. Not only does Gutierrez challenge the status quo, but he also seems unshaken in the midst of all the anti-liberationists who challenge liberation theology.

Anti-liberationists from many perspectives rage at liberation theologians. Theologians like Rene De Visme Williamson use the classical hermeneutic interpretation of the Bible to say that liberty is not the focal point of the Bible; that equality is not a Kingdom of God ideal; that subversive revolutionary activity is explicitly not allowed; and that one of the most useful teachings of the Bible is how to live in adversity.[106] W. Dayton Roberts, another anti-liberationist, asserts that class struggle is not present in the Bible, but rather spiritual warfare between the demonic and the divine.[107] Roberts goes on to blast liberation theology for politicizing the gospel message; for equating spiritual salvation with good works thus making salvation a moral atonement; substituting works for spirituality; confusing values resulting from the Marxist class analysis; not relying on the Holy Spirit with the emphasis on human responsibility for changing the world; and for a flagrant misunderstanding of scripture.[108] Ronald Nash goes on to say that liberation theology should avoid Marxist, socialistic, and communistic systems because they have failed miserably to eliminate human suffering. Instead Nash believes a liberation critique within capitalism would best serve the relief from oppression.[109]

Walter W. Benjamin continues the anti-liberationist rhetoric by saying liberation theologians have been silent about the misery of socialist economic systems in Eastern Europe. Benjamin's visit to Eastern Europe before 1989 revealed the opposite of the Kingdom of God ideals liberationists promise, instead he found "depression, resignation, alienation, anger, and suspicion."[110] Charles R. Strain puts liberation theology in the genre category of a secular ideology, and argues that it is similar to theology genres that "occlude self-critical reflection."[111] In other words liberation theologians jumped into a genre category without employing self-critical reflection to consider how this focused their analysis.

Thomas G. Sanders says that liberation theology has a false notion that history is a "progressive unfolding of moral aspirations," because the Bible supports the notion of a "permanent dialectic between the hopes of mankind and the contradictions that undermine them."[112] Sanders also warns against the absolutistic notions of utopianism, which rest on strict categories of good vs. bad, oppressed vs. liberation, etc. In other words, Sanders is suspicious of liberation theology because it makes absolute distinctions about what is good and what is evil. Yet, Gutierrez and all the other liberation theologians continue to proclaim their theology in the face of massive opposition from the church, Latin American governments, and the international community that seeks to protect their economic interests.

In conclusion, proposition five gives us the spiritual side of liberation theology. Gutierrez stresses the vertical and horizontal relationships of the Christian faith. Conversion, for Gutierrez, consists of opening up to God and humanity in such a way that incorporates spirituality and political involvement. In essence, Gutierrez extends spiritual salvation to include salvation from de-humanized economic, social, and political structures. He draws the parallel of individuals taking part in the Eucharist in every aspect of life, in other words a total sharing of common substance. Religiously, this means that the laity should be empowered with voice and authority, yet the Vatican rejects many of these notions by labeling them Marxist.

Many anti-liberationists groups in both the Protestant and Catholic groups blast liberation theologians from various perspectives. Many Protestants consider liberation theology to be heretical due to thematic extensions of spiritual salvation into economic, social, and political spheres of life. Class analysis is also considered to be a non-Biblical theme that results in mixing Marxist values with Christian ideals. And the notion of a progressive evolution of human emancipation is rejected in light of the ongoing Biblical dialectic between good and evil.

CONCLUSION

The classical hermeneutic allowed us to interpret the propositional structure of Gustavo Gutierrez's A Theology of Liberation, which in turn allowed us to view the intricate rhetorical strategies Gutierrez used to launch his propositions of liberation theology over sixteen years ago. By combining this publication with other liberation publications a more holistic account of liberation theology was provided. The rest of our tools provided a context of inter-perspective dialogue with these publications. These tools also helped us to understand the type of European philosophy that influences liberation thinkers. The double-edged sword of applying this same philosophy on the movement it influenced provides an excellent introductory base of analysis. Chapter six will conclude this analysis.

Chapter Five

Conclusion

INTRODUCTION

This introduction to liberation theology is just a beginning. We allowed a variety of texts to speak from many different perspectives. The purpose of this closing chapter will be to provide a self-critical evaluation of our analysis; to provide a brief summary of our tools and what they tell us; to perspectivize liberation theology in the global arena; and to provide a personal evaluation of liberation theology.

PERSPECTIVIZING

Perspectivizing is an intervention of one structure upon another.[1] Thus, using different philosophic systems and points of view on the topic of liberation theology really means that multiple interpretive structures have been imposed on the texts of liberation theology. The resulting interpretations are at least once removed from the phenomena in such a way that the interpretations of liberation theology texts do not completely embody the original texts. Logically, this points to the notion that the analyst can never escape the discursive power of language by critical evaluation.[2] Thus, at best we can only participate in a dialogue between perspectives, without forgetting that it is impossible to escape from the realm of language and symbols in our role as a critic.

Due to these limitations, it seems that our tools have served us well. The unique compilation of philosophic approaches yields multiple interpretations from significant perspectives. In this way the analysis models the phenomena for us so that the reader can participate in a dialogue from a multitude of perspectives. After the reader participates in the dialogue context, s/he experiences some of the flavor of those texts. The addition of more tools would increase the analysis base and would allow the participant more probing descriptions. Thus, the five philosophic approaches of phenomenology, hermeneutics, structuralism, semiotics, and semantics have served us well. In essence, the combination of these five philosophic approaches has enabled us to interpret the texts of liberation theology in a fashion that gives a close approximation of the phenomena of liberation theology. These approximations have been shown to be reasonable, descriptive, reflective, holistic, and intuitive.

Yet, we have only provided an introduction as the breadth of the texts contained within the body of liberation theology is overwhelming. There continues to be a huge amount of literature produced on this topic, and the publications are written from a wide variety of perspectives. This situation forces one to pick and choose publications selectively. Thus, this introduction just starts with the analysis, rather than finishing it. At best it provides a base for the reader to continue the analysis. Now let us look at what each philosophic domain has told us.

PHENOMENOLOGY

The two analytical tools drawn from phenomenology allowed us to focus on both the propositions of A Theology of Liberation and the texts within the liberation theology arena. The focusing, or bracketing, was always done with a perspective. For example, the classical hermeneutic perspective was used as the first approach to interpret the propositions of Gutierrez's book above. This bracketing allowed us to interpret this book within the domain of its immediate context. But, whenever we switched perspectives another set of boundaries was used to interpret the same text. Thus, the phenomenological epoche allowed us to focus on the texts of liberation theology with each of the other perspectives.

The advantage of using this epoche, or bracketing, is realized in the reflexivity it offers the analysis. In other words, the phenomenological epoche always offers an immediate reference that perspectivizes our analysis. For example, the classical hermeneutic used to bracket A Theology of Liberation immediately warns the readers that a perspective was used in the analysis. It also allows the analysis to be verified by going back and tracing the procedures of analysis. This type of openness about how the analysis was accomplished is very helpful in a number of ways.

First, it reveals that a perspective was used to analyze the data. This openness helps the reader understand the basis of the analysis, which, as we have mentioned earlier, is always founded on a perspective. This avoids the pitfalls of presenting our findings as facts in the erroneous manner of positivistic science. Second, the phenomenological epoche can be traced so that the reader can track down and verify the findings in the analysis according to the boundaries of the perspective. This ability opens up the analysis for scholarly criticism. Third, the phenomenological epoche humanizes us in that the interpretations and descriptions of phenomena are always shown to be using the data in such a way that the original phenomena is re-contextualized by the perspectives used in the analysis. This notion helps us to always remember that our analysis is at least once removed from the phenomena, which points to the impossibility of ever giving a perfect, or a completely descriptive analysis. This realization should humble us, and make us less inclined to marginalize and categorize the individuals we analyze.

The second use of phenomenology allowed us to view the consciousness of individuals according to what they were attending to. For example, the modern age industrial expansionism into Latin America was viewed as a great profit making venture by Western Europeans in the seventeenth and eighteenth centuries. But, the same activity was viewed as a massive social, cultural, political, and religious enslavement by Latin Americans, who viewed industrial expansionism as an encroachment upon their territory. The phenomenological critique of human experience allows this type of plural interpretation of the same phenomena, thus making possible a more holistic account of the audience surrounding liberation discourse.

HERMENEUTICS

The three hermeneutics served us very well in our description of liberation theology rhetoric. The classical hermeneutic allowed us to interpret A Theology of Liberation from its own context, which allowed Gutierrez the opportunity to speak to us from the context of his own book. It is only fair to allow the participants in the rhetorical discourse as much opportunity to speak as possible, and the classical hermeneutic enables the analyst to do this. The following is a brief summary of these findings.

Gutierrez believes that theology always changes thus he wants liberation theology to represent the current historical theological evolutionary stage. He also secularized the kingdom of God by making humans responsible for establishing the kingdom of God on earth. Thus, Gutierrez uses the second greatest commandment of Jesus to "love your neighbor as yourself" to critique all social, economic, political, and religious structures on earth. For Gutierrez, the extension of this commandment into all aspects of life will bring about the kingdom of God on earth. This extension results in a desire to establish democratic socialism that shares the wealth of the earth so that everyone has the necessities of life, which means poverty will be eliminated.

Another result of this "new hermeneutic," which critiques societies structures with Jesus' second greatest commandment to "love your neighbor as yourself," is the goal of empowering the laity of the Catholic Church with a voice over everything that affects their lives. In essence, Gutierrez wants the laity to be responsible for their faith in such a way that the professional clergy are at best only participants in the believing community. The above are examples of how the classical hermeneutic allowed us to understand Gutierrez's liberation theology.

The other two hermeneutics allowed us the ability to break the boundaries of the classical hermeneutic. The philosophical hermeneutic allowed us to view Gutierrez's extension of the second greatest commandment into all areas of life as an attempt for the Catholic Church to regain the vitality it has lost in Latin America. The classical hermeneutic allowed us to view this activity as Gutierrez's plea for genuine Christianity to be adopted by the Catholic Church. Yet the philosophical hermeneutic allows us to interpret this plea as an attempt for the Catholic Church to become legitimate in the concrete lived-experience of Latin American Christians.

The critical hermeneutic allows us to interpret poverty as a key ingredient in the consciousness formation of societies.   In essence, Gutierrez challenges poverty as being non-Christian, which means it must be eradicated. The extension of the second greatest commandment into the economic realm allows us to understand how Gutierrez challenges poverty. Basically liberation theologians are trying to re-educate the masses of poor people with their conscientization projects, which are manifested in grass-root Christian organizations. These organizations help people become conscious of their exploitative situation and then to take concrete action based on Biblical morality to eliminate the newly recognized problems. The critical hermeneutic gives us a glimpse of the hopelessness of the poor, and of Gutierrez's attempt to establish hope in a future society that will be free from poverty. The hopeless consciousness is viewed as fatalistic, but the consciousness of the grass-root Christian communities has hope, which can be seen in political challenges to the status quo.

STRUCTURALISM

The poststructuralist perspective allows us yet another interpretation of this extension of the second greatest commandment. It allows us to interpret this activity as an attempt to empower the masses of poverty stricken people with the power of voice. This happens in the political realm with the ability to vote; it happens also in the religious realm with the laity taking up the responsibility for all the aspects of their Christian faith; and in the economic realm by enabling the poor to gain the basic necessities of life from a profit sharing socialistic economic system. This empowering would reduce the hold of the coercive political leaders, the Catholic hierarchy, and those who would profit from the international capitalistic economic system if democratic socialism succeeds.   Thus, post-structuralism helps us to interpret liberation theology as a massive power struggle that seeks to empower the masses of poor people while at the same time decreasing the power of the ruling minorities.

Moreover, the structuralist notion of "transformation" allows us to plot how liberation theologians are attempting to achieve the empowering of the poor. Transformations are structural propositions that in effect change social structures. For example, when Gutierrez labels poverty as a sin, he is importing a transformational proposition into the social structures that have allowed poverty to exist. When poverty is regarded as a sin it challenges the existing political, economic, and religious structures that have permitted this situation in the past. It challenges the church to extend the second greatest commandment into the economic arena, it challenges the economic system to establish socialistic profit sharing policies, and it challenges the political structures to give the masses more power to vote on national policies that affect their lives.

SEMIOTICS

This philosophic approach gave us a host of tools to use in our analysis. The concept of "sign" was used in every step of the analysis. For example, the grammatical structure of Gutierrez's book was the sign pointing to the immediate context of his propositions, and their supporting justifications, examples, and results. The "syntagmatic" aspect allowed to read this book according to the linear scheme of the words, sentences, and paragraphs.   The "paradigmatic" allowed us to interpret the vertical possibilities of Gutierrez's book. For example, when Gutierrez secularized the kingdom of God he gave humans the responsibility for its establishment. Yet, a paradigmatic interpretation points to Gutierrez defending God from being the author of corrupt governmental systems.   This is a vertical interpretation of the syntagmatic chain referring to the immediate context of secularization.

The "synchronic" allowed us to visualize the poverty context of Latin America in the moment of the twentieth century, and the "diachronic" allowed us to understand the significant events through time that fostered this situation.   "Text" was used to label the participants and written products of the liberation movement. One of these texts included the Pope, who is considered a progressive right wing opponent of liberation theology. Basically, Pope John Paul II supports the human rights issues of liberation theology, but he rejects the notion of Marxist class analysis that is used to analyze the Latin American context. He believes Marxist class analysis and the idea of class struggle would be dangerous if assimilated into the Latin American Church.   He also completely rejects the militant violence associated with Marxist class analysis, and warns liberation theologians not to adopt secular ideological methods of violence for creating social change. "Intertextuality" allowed us to fit liberation theology with the major texts of its immediate context. It allowed us to interpret liberation theology from a number of perspectives including the poor people of Latin America, who have much to gain if liberation themes are implemented and actually work on national levels; the international economic systems of multinational corporations who are embedded with the governments of Latin America; the United States that seeks to protect American economic and military interests by at times using the noble "freedom and democracy" themes as a front for less noble motives; and the Catholic Church, which views the Marxist aspects of liberation theology as being dangerous and unholy, and which is threatened by the idea of the laity being empowered with a religious voice because this would make the Catholic clergy more and more redundant outside the context of base-Christian communities.

A "metatextual" analysis allowed us to focus on any of the above texts in order to determine how they functioned outside of the immediate textual boundaries. For example, liberation theology as a whole can be seen as a group of Catholic Priests who want to "do something" to eliminate the poverty of the Third World. Thus, the whole movement can be seen as an attempt to do something about poverty, which becomes a central focus around which everything else such as the Christian faith, the role of the Catholic Church, the role of the Priests, and the political, economic, and social realms are all re-contextualized.

SEMANTICS

The semantic labeling of propositions allowed us to provide an interpretative propositional outline of Gutierrez's book, A Theology of Liberation. This was a very straightforward way to organize and label Gutierrez's arguments for establishing his liberation theology. This also became the springboard from which we used the other perspectives of our tools to analyze and expand the basic propositions of Gutierrez's book. This kept the analysis organized and focused.

The perspectives based approach to determining meaning was one of the foundation stones of our analysis. This granted us the ability to legitimize a plurality of interpretations based on different perspectives. This concept also gave foundation to the notion of a "dialogue between perspectives," which, in essence, is what we accomplished in this book. For example, a post-structuralist perspective would give legitimate interpretations of who is being empowered by liberation theology propositions. Yet, the classical hermeneutic didn't allow us to mention any empowering activity in Gutierrez's book because it was outside of the classical hermeneutic boundaries to do so unless empowering was specifically mentioned by Gutierrez. Thus, we could only interpret meaning according to the perspectives we used in the specific stage of analysis.

Taken together, all five philosophic approaches of phenomenology, hermeneutics, structuralism, semiotics, and semantics gave us a set of tools that allow creative interpretive dialogue among liberation related texts. Each approach gave us tools that enabled us to provide a holistic, descriptive, reflective, intuitive, and reasonable analysis of liberation theology.

In conclusion, our tools allow a unique interpretation of liberation theology texts; yet in essence each perspective re-structured the phenomena. This points out the impossibility of escaping the discursive power of language, as an ideological critique becomes another ideology. Thus at best one can only create a dialogue between perspectives and texts in such a way that the texts can be experienced by readers sufficiently to allow them to understand the phenomenon under analysis and to draw their own conclusions about it. Now for perspectivizing liberation theology in the global arena.

THE GLOBAL PERSPECTIVE

Father Edward Cleary, a Jesuit priest who spoke on liberation theology at Ohio University in Athens, Ohio in the Spring of 1987, said the total population of people who support liberation theology is two million, with about one hundred liberation theologians. In global population terms this movement is not very significant, yet the eight hundred and fifty martyrs of this movement since 1970 indicate the strong reaction this movement has generated within the Latin American context. Also, the 1986 decision of the U.S. Catholic bishops to opt for the poor demonstrates the prospectively high level of influence this movement may wield. However, all the power and persuasiveness of the movement should not disguise its failings.

Basically, liberation theologians are considered naive for adopting the Marxist class analysis for their "scientific" view of Latin American reality. The Catholic hierarchy, as well as the governments of Latin America have strongly resisted this analysis. In essence, the use of Marxist analysis, and the secularization of the kingdom of God, have proved to be two extremely negative elements of this movement. The general notion concerning Marxism is that it is not scientific, because every country that has chosen to operate from a Marxist base is further from being liberated than capitalistic countries. And the attempt to secularize the kingdom of God rests on a questionable notion that humanity operates from a progressive evolutionary consciousness base, which has no historical support.[3] Thus, Marxist analysis and the secularization of the kingdom of God have given liberation theology a negative orientation. Ideally, the future transformations of this movement will eventually support the implementation of world humanism and move away from Marxist and secularization efforts.

Regardless of the negative elements of liberation theology, this movement will eventually enable more poor people to enjoy the basics of life to which they are entitled. This will result from both the conscientization projects and the establishment of base-Christian communities in Latin America. Raising the consciousness of the masses of poor people, which will eventually make them a political entity, will force governments to grant more concessions that will enable the poor to raise their living standards. This will work because the base-Christian movements will enable many poor people to experience what the conscientization projects are propagating. Thus, the combination of conscientization projects with the practical implementation of base-Christian communities will eventually work in creating a political force out of the poor masses that can be mobilized toward establishing basic socialistic goals.

Orbis Books of Maryknoll, New York continues to publish liberation theology literature in the United States, but since the fall of Eastern Europe in 1989 socialism of any kind will have a very difficult time being seriously heard in the U.S. Thus, the liberation theology literature will less and less effect on the Catholic majority of laity in Latin American, and on North American Christians through Orbis' publishing efforts. The basic game plan now is to use economic systems that generate a better economic life for the countries using it. Democratic capitalism seems to be winning in the debates as the system that helps more people when it is utilized.

In conclusion, the liberation theology movement is small in terms of the population who follow it, but it is very powerful in creating strong reactions of violence from its opposition. It also contains strong transformational propositions that have led to wide assimilation of many of its ideals. Yet there is an overriding negative side to this movement due to its inclusion of Marx's class analysis, and its call for the secularization of the kingdom of God. Yet these negative aspects may not hinder the positive political transformations this movement will have on the global community due to the conscientization projects and the base-Christian organizations, along with the publishing efforts of Orbis Books.

PERSONAL CONCLUSION

Interest in liberation theology is a result of my desire to participate in international Christian missionary activity. The specific type of missionary service of Bible translation and literacy development among pre-literate societies pointed me into some type of Third World setting where liberation theology is very strong. As an evangelical Christian I believe that the Bible as God's Word is authoritative over every other world-view perspective.[4] Thus for all the different ways that we have viewed liberation theology the final analysis for me rests in whether it can be supported from the texts of the scripture. Thus, my conservative evangelical Christian world-view guides the following thoughts.

I agree in part with Ron Sider, who says that the Bible posits God being on the side of the poor from the examples of the Exodus, the Prophets, and the ministry of Jesus.[5] Yet I also believe that the wealthy can participate in this option for the poor by using their resources to humanize poverty stricken groups of people. In essence, I feel that God is on the side of humanity,[6] and that He has chosen to give vivid examples of speaking for the poor in the Exodus account, and in the ministry of Jesus, in order to demonstrate the continual need not to forget the poor. Thus, restricting God's concern only for the poor and not for all of humanity is a mistake. I'm also very concerned about the nature of liberation in the texts of liberation theology.

According to the Biblical account, God's primary liberation is from sin, death and lies; a liberation to love in an unlovable environment.[7] "Sin" refers to humanities rebellion and fall from our right-standing relationship with God and His principles, which in effect is the major cause of all our problems on this planet. "Lies" refer to de-humanized notions of security and significance. For example, one could plot the political decisions of leaders who chose false-security that resulted in de-humanized policies. For example, Chairman Mao of China has been interpreted as opting for political security over his opponent Chou Enlai with the cultural revolution, which lasted from 1966 to 1976. The massive destruction of this revolution within China is replete with examples of every form of de-humanized behavior. Yet one of God's primary ministries is to satisfy the human desire for security. God does this with notions of eternal life, which offers a solution for physical death, and with demonstrations of sacrificial love that are signs pointing to the great value of individuals. Yet, God also offers solutions of significance.

God offers escape to individuals who are enslaved in serving their egos. Belief in God provides a new center of focus, which shifts from focusing on the self to focusing on the Creator. This new focus releases individuals and allows them to become more other-centered. This other-centeredness allows one to enjoy sacrificial giving, which reverses the greed and selfish tendencies in a way that a person can find satisfaction in appropriately serving and giving to others. In essence, this other-centeredness provides a new framework in which to live. Thus, by combining the notions of liberation from sin and death with liberation from de-humanized world-views of significance and security, the foundations for a liberation theology can be established for a global liberation of economic, social, political, and religious structures. Yet, the following question persists: Why hasn't the two-thousand year old ministry of Jesus Christ produced liberation from false significance and security, and thus a liberation from de-humanized economic, social, political, and religious structures?

The answer is that all people on this planet are engaged in a massive spiritual war that pits the demonic forces of Satan against the heavenly forces of God. Everyone on this planet is caught up in this war either aware or unaware. People who loose this war tend to make life miserable on themselves and everyone around them. Thus, the ongoing problems of political, military, and economic power structures are spiritually based. Also, the most important liberation God provides is a personal liberation from sin. Jesus satisfies all of God's justice requirements when He took our sins away on the cross. The renewal of a right relationship with God is the foundation upon which all liberation rests. Once saved a person has the moral and ethical motivation and power to live in liberated ways that often leads to the type of material, political, and economic liberation that liberation theologians write about. Christians who worship God together, pray for and serve each other and their communities, work hard and smart, act in moral and ethical ways, and who continue doing these things tend to find all sorts of liberation in their lives over time.

Yet there doesn't seem to be a progressive evolution of human consciousness that builds on the liberation of previous generations. In essence, every generation, and each individual, is responsible for accepting and practicing liberation from de-humanized world-views. I hold that liberation from de-humanized behavior is very possible within each generation, but I don't believe it can progress unless each generation decides to follow liberation principles. There is no evidence of any nation, group, or family line that provides enough evidence to convince me otherwise. Yet this pessimism is countered by a strong faith that individuals and groups can be liberated in any age if they so desire. For example, look at the economic liberation Japan has experienced since WWII. But what about those who do not desire to follow the path of liberation?

The answer to this question brings us into the political and economic realm. Some individuals will choose to live by God's principles, and some will choose to live in self-centered de-humanized ways. Those who follow along the path of money and military power will usually follow de-humanized principles of greed, selfishness, and servitude to their ego. Liberation theologians who attempt to re-structure society under the umbrella of "loving your neighbor as yourself" will have little effect on those who decide not to participate. Plus more people will be killed who attempt to implement this re-structuring upon the unwilling. Those in power will not re-distribute their wealth to the masses of people because they will not trust themselves to the masses afterwards when they have to live with them on the same level. Thus, Marxist class struggle will not be possible without many people getting killed. And liberation theologians will not be able to implement their classless re-structuring without taking up military warfare.

But, the notion of a classless society is bogus. Indeed, the few remaining communist countries that boast of their classless society are lying because they don't have one. The notion of a classless society is propaganda fiction. My doubts about establishing a classless society also make me doubt the possibility of a complete socialistic sharing of wealth. Therefore, I don't believe that the liberation theology ideal of a complete democratic socialism will succeed. If they want to keep a type of socialism it should be adjusted into working for the basics of life for everyone while allowing a free market to operate. In other words, liberation theologians should not attempt to re-structure the economic, social, political, and religious structures of society under their socialistic interpretation of the second greatest commandment. They should rather work within the current system and take a patient and safer political approach of appealing to the basic necessities for everyone. And they should pay serious attention to the failed socialistic experiments around the world before insisting on socialism as a viable option.

I first became interested in studying liberation theology in the mid 80s. At first democratic socialism seemed the best economic system that would serve to liberate the world with the basics of life. Then from 1987-1988 my wife and I lived and worked in the People's Republic of China where we observed totalitarian socialism being practiced.[8] After seeing the effects of this system I'm convinced that socialism as a whole only produces economic nightmares.[9] Compared with the small free-market projects within the PROC, which were characterized by motivated, creative, and energetic workers, the socialized state businesses were complete economic and motivational failures. The PROC is a very wealthy country with smart and intelligent people. If ever their leadership decides to put into practice a political and economic system that would embellish and release the efforts of their people the world will quickly start learning Mandarin Chinese! As long as the basic religious, political, and economic freedoms are denied the people of the PROC they will continue to squander in their self-inflicted poverty. Liberation theologians who still fight for democratic socialism need to demonstrate one solid and sustained economic system that has achieved measurable economic and material liberation for the masses of poor people before they continue propagating a system that has up to this time failed miserably to liberate anyone.

Another fundamental issue here is whether liberation theologians are correct in secularizing the kingdom of God. Jesus was accused by the Jewish leaders of plotting to destroy the man-made Jerusalem temple with a heavenly temple made by God, (Mark 14:58). The fundamental issue is whether such messages like this are metaphoric examples of God's will for his followers to implement on earth. In other words, if the kingdom of God is earth-centered as post-millennial eschatology suggests, then believers are responsible for changing the world to fit Biblical ideals. If this is true, then liberation theologians are on target with some of their activities. But there is much dispute over the millennial question. Post-millennialism is not widely held. A heavenly based kingdom of God checks participation in earth centered utopian goals. Thus working to change the global structures to fit the patterns of the kingdom of God is a mistake from a pre-millennial and amillennial perspective.[10] Yet Christians are to apply kingdom principles in every sphere of their lives, but only God has the ability and power to pull off a global liberation that liberation theologians write about. A (pre-)(a-)millennial view of Christian eschatology says this will happen at Jesus' second coming, but not until then!

Yet one of the most effective political activities liberation theologians could take would be to encourage current political regimes to adopt and implement policies that will grant the masses of poor people all the basics of life. This could be a positive campaign that would encourage the political leaders to establish stability from revolutionary ideologies by raising the quality of life of everyone in their nations. Thus, instead of spending all the national resources on the military and lining their own pockets with grafted money, these leaders could be shown the benefits of political stability that goes along with a social structure that provides public access to all the basics of life. This type of transformational process could be much more effective than the current policy of always proclaiming what the government is not doing.

In conclusion, my evangelical Christianity guides my interpretation of liberation theology. For me, God is on the side of humanity, with the Biblical emphasis on the poor being a check against the tendency to marginalize this group. Liberation from sin and death is the primary liberation target for Jesus, along with liberation from de-humanized world views of significance and security. There is no evidence for the progressive evolution of human consciousness, thus the need remains to choose liberation ideals in every generation. In light of the present spiritual warfare the best strategy for liberation theologians, (besides preaching a liberating gospel message!), is to work to gain the basic necessities of life for everyone. Thus, they need to re-think their strategy of global democratic socialism due to the massive failure socialism has had on countries that have used it. It seems best to target on getting the basics of life for everyone, and possibly implementing a positive campaign focusing on the political stability of satisfying the masses with the basics of life. Yet, this will require a re-examination of secularizing the kingdom of God which for many conservative Christians is a mistaken and an unachievable post-millennial utopian goal.

CONCLUSION

Liberation theology is a very rich and extensive religious movement. It continues to teach the Christian community a tremendous amount of lessons. Marxism and Christianity are viewed as the main sources for liberation theology, as liberation theologians have assimilated Marxist economics and class analysis into the gospel message. Coupled with the secularization of the kingdom of God, this assimilation process, which was created out of the Marxist Christian dialogue, has resulted into a powerful theological and ideological movement that has challenged the world's economic, social, political, and religious structures. Liberation theologians basically want to transform society into following the kingdom of God ideal of "loving your neighbor as yourself." Their themes of care and concern for the poor are supported worldwide. Yet, many doubt the validity of liberation theology in their radical re-contextualizing of the historic Christian faith. They have adopted Marxist analysis too quickly and have found themselves serving a system that breeds more poverty than it eliminates. Yet liberation theologians who live in the Third World have put their lives on the line for their views. Even though mistaken I cannot help but love and admire them for their courage and devotion, and for raising my awareness for the poor.

Yet, let us learn from liberation theologians to be wary of leaving the historic Christian faith. The faith that speaks of Jesus' resurrection into an eternally liberated and abundant life. His liberation for us provides the motivation and power to live liberated and abundant lives on earth. By first being liberated from the sin that separates us from God, and then being empowered to live out liberated lives on earth through the power of His indwelling Holy Spirit we can change this world for the better! His Spirit and Word will also help us discern the right ways to live, the best economic and political systems that will liberate, and the motivation to patiently endure when the situation is less than perfect. Ron Nash rightly sums up what is needed:

> The poor need caring Christians to describe and encourage the kinds of economic and political institutions that really will deliver the poor from poverty and free the oppressed from tyranny. The best hope for these people is a combination of a free market economy and limited constitutional government which can serve as the foundation for a new liberation theology, a true liberation theology - one that offers genuine hope for economic and political liberation. But every human being in the world also has a right to expect self-described Christian theologians to proclaim the New Testament gospel and its message of liberation from sin. Until liberation theologians begin to do all this, their system will continue to lead, not toward liberation, but to slavery.[11]

NOTES

Chapter One, Background - Notes

1. Edward Cleary, a Dominican Priest, traced the roots of this strategy to the Aristotelian notion of "see, judge, do". Also, Thomas Aquinas made this popular by his scientific treatment of Christian theology. Cleary spoke on liberation theology in Latin America at Ohio University, Athens, Ohio, May 12, 1987.
2. Washington Gladden, "The New Evangel" ed. Paul H. Boase The Rhetoric of Christian Socialism (New York: Random House, 1969) 128.
3. T. Howland Sanks, S.J. "Liberation Theology and the Social Gospel: Variations on a Theme" Theological Studies, Dec. 1980:668-682.
   In this article Sanks develops the dis/similarities between liberation theology (LT) and the social gospel (SG). In essence, Sanks says "theology is necessarily conditioned by the social situation", and thinks this is correct, (p.668). He goes on to say that Walter Rauschenbusch identified themes of injustice and oppression 50 years earlier in a different social setting, thus the similarity of LT and SG. But, there are differences, such as: Massive international exploitation in the Third World by the First World, a situation unlike America's SG setting; predominate Roman Catholicism in LT as opposed to protestantism in SG; LT tendency to take radical social and economic reform action as opposed to "democratic" extension into the economic realm in SG; LT is "more sophisticated in their understanding and critique of ideologies than were the Social Gospel theologians" (p.681); and lastly Sanks believes LT is has more "theological vision" than the SG movement.
4. For a full discussion of the background of each of these participants see: Rosino Gibellini, ed., Frontiers of Theology in Latin America (Maryknoll, New York: Orbis Books, 1979) 305-318.
5. Leonardo Boff, and Clodovis Boff, Salvation and Liberation (Maryknoll, New York: Orbis Books, 1984) 2.
6. Boff, 1984, p.2.
7. Gustavo Gutierrez, "Liberation Praxis and Christian Faith" ed. Rosino Gibellini, Frontiers of Theology in Latin America (Maryknoll, New York: Orbis Books, 1979) 1-2.
8. Arthur F. McGovern, Marxism: An American Christian Perspective (Maryknoll, New York: Orbis Books, 1984) 177.
9. Boff, 1984, p.3.
10. Boff, 1984, p.10.
11. Leonardo Boff, Church: Charism and Power (New York: Crossroad, 1985) 131-137.
12. Black Theology Project, "Message to The Black Church and Community" eds. Gerald H. Anderson, and Thomas F. Stransky, Mission Trends No.4, 1979:127. This is an excerpt from a very significant Black theology conference held in Atlanta, Ga., August 1977.
   Rosemary Ruether is a key writer for the feminist liberation movement. Her article: "Crisis in Sex and Race: Black Theology vs. Feminist Theology" outlines "oppression" stemming from "white male domination", it appears on pages 175-187 in Mission Trends No. 4.
13. McGovern 179.
14. Raul Vidales, "Methodological Issues in Liberation Theology" in Frontier of Theology in Latin America, 44-57.

15. McGovern, 172.

16. McGovern, 172-173.

17. Of course Moses didn't rewrite theology, opt for socialism, etc., but he did allow God to use him to help liberate the Hebrews out of Egypt, thus qualifying as a "basic" liberator.

18. Clyde M. Woods, The Living Way Commentary On the Old Testament (Shreveport, Louisiana: Lambert Book House, 1972) 1.

19. McGovern, 174.

20. McGovern, 174-175.

21. Rosino Gibellini, (ed.) Frontiers of Theology in Latin America (Maryknoll, New York: Orbis Books, 1979) 305-321. Here is where the biographical information of liberation theologians are found including their background, training, and major published works.

22. Enrique Dussel, History and the Theology of Liberation (Maryknoll, New York: Orbis Books, 1976) 111-113.

Gerald M. Fagin, S.J. (ed.), Vatican II (Wilmington, Delaware: Michael Glazier, Inc., 1984).

23. Dussel, 113-116.
      McGovern, 176-177.

24. Dussel, 113.

25. Dussel, 113-116.

26. McGovern, 177.

27. Thomas G. Sanders, "The Theology of Liberation: Christian Utopianism," Christianity and Crisis 17 Sept. 1973:167.

28. McGovern, 222.

29. McGovern, 210-238.

30. Beverly Wildung Harrison, "Challenging the Western Paradigm: "The Theology in the Americas" Conference," Christianity and Crisis 27 Oct. 1975:251.

31. McGovern, 1984,pp.202. Another book detailing the significance of this meeting is: John Eagleson, & Philip Scharper, (eds), Puebla and Beyond (Maryknoll, New York: Orbis Books, 1979).

32. McGovern, 202.

33. Grant Osborne, "Theologians from North, South, and Central America Gather in Mexico" Christianity Today 13 Jan. 1984:60+.

34. Leslie R. Keylock, "The Vatican Tries to Rein In a Leading Proponent of Liberation Theology" Christianity Today 19 Oct. 1984:46-47.

35. Keylock, 46.

36. "Pope Nears End of Tour," The Athens Messenger 12 Ap. 1987:A-3.

37. Humberto Belli, & Ronald Nash, Beyond Liberation Theology. (Grand Rapids, Michigan: Baker, 1992) 53.

38. Father Edward Cleary, a Dominican Priest who is Professor of Pastoral Theology at the Pontifical College Josephinum in Columbus, Ohio, said in 1987 that there would not be a major split among liberation theologians and the traditional Catholic hierarchy in the future. He said that liberation theologians have already been accepted into the existing structure of the Catholic Church, thus there is no need to break away. Yet I feel that the most radical liberation theologians will continue to break out of the Catholic Church like Leonardo Boff did in 1992.

39. Quentin L. Quade, The Pope and Revolution (Washington, D.C.: Ethics and Public Policy Center, 1982) 1.

40. Quade, 47.

41. "Liberation Troubles" Christian Century 12-19 Sept. 1984:826-827.

42. Thomas Niehaus, and Brady Tyson, "The Catholic Right in Contemporary Brazil: The Case of the Society for the Defense of Tradition, Family, and Property (TEP)" eds. Lyle C. Brown, and William F. Copper, Religion in Latin American Life and Literature (Waco, Texas: Markham Press Fund, 1980) 394-409.

43. Jeffrey K. Hadden, "Taking Stock of the New Christian Right" Christianity Today 13 Jn. 1986:38-39.

44. Niehaus and Tyson, 408.

45. Anthony Campolo, Partly Right (Waco, Texas: Word Books, 1985) 211-212.

46. Campolo, 216-217.

47. This is my own perception of what most U.S. citizens believe.

48. Paul G. King, and David O. Woodyard, The Journey Toward Freedom: Economic Structures and Theological Perspectives (London: Associated University Press, 1982) 59.

49. King & Woodyard, 63.

50. King & Woodyard, 82.

51. The U.S. symbols and statements of "In God We Trust, Democracy, Freedom, Justice, etc.," are very beautiful, true, and right. I support these notions completely as a patriot of the United States. Yet anything that is true can be used as a camouflage to cover up wicked behavior, and at times the U.S. is guilty of this in its foreign policies. And as a text in the metatextual analysis of liberation theology the United States is both a champion and opponent of freedom, democracy, & justice.

52. McGovern, 173.

53. Sergio Torres, and John Eagleson, eds., The Challenge of Basic Christian Communities (Maryknoll, New York: Orbis Books, 1980) 19.

54. Gibellini, 307-313.

55. Karl Marx, "For a Ruthless Criticism of Everything Existing," ed. Robert C. Tucker, The Marx-Engels Reader (London: W.W. Norton & Company, 1978) 15.

56. Joseph Kroger, "Prophetic-Critical and Practical-Strategic Tasks of Theology: Habermas and Liberation Theology" Theological Studies no. 46, 1985:5.

57. Kroger, 8.

58. Kroger, 16.

59. Martin Jay, The Dialectical Imagination (Boston: Little, Brown, and Company, 1973) xvi.

60. Jay, 41.

61. Kroger, 8.

62. Gustavo Gutierrez, A Theology of Liberation (Maryknoll, New York: Orbis Books, 1973) 13-14.

Chapter Two, Marxism - Notes

1. Arthur F. McGovern, Marxism: An American Christian Perspective (Maryknoll, New York: Orbis Books, 1984) 11. This text will be our main source for the historical sketch of Marxism.

2. McGovern, 32.

3. Oscar Romero, A Martyr's Message of Hope (Kansas City, Missouri: Celebration Books, 1981) 170.

4. Russell Bradner Norris, God, Marx, and the Future (Philadelphia: Fortress Press, 1974) 2.

5. Ben W. Morse, and Lynn A. Phelps, Interpersonal Communication: A Relational Perspective (Minneapolis, Minnesota: Burgess Publishing Company, 1980) 334. This paradigm was to indicate the interaction of self-disclosure, trust, feedback, and empathy. Dr. Phelps indicated that this paradigm is not original, it came from the articles in Chapter Seven entitled "Towards Relational Escalation" in the above book.

6. John R. W. Stott, "The Biblical Basis of Evangelism" in Mission Trends No. 2, ed. by Gerald H. Anderson, and Thomas F. Stransky, (Toronto: Paulist Press, 1975) 14.

7. Rodger Garaudy, and Quentin Lauer, S.J., A Christian - Communist Dialogue (Garden City, New York: Doubleday & Company, Inc., 1968) 8.

8. Garaudy & Lauer, 9.

9. Norris, 2.

10. Marvin K. Mayers, Christianity Confronts Culture (Grand Rapids, Michigan: Zondervan Publishing House, 1974) 57.

11. Mayers, 60.

12. S.J. Samartha, "Dialogue as a Continuing Christian Concern", in Mission Trends No. 1, ed. by Gerald H. Anderson, and Thomas F. Stransky, (Toronto: Paulist Press, 1974) 253.

13. Peter Beyerhaus, "Mission and Humanization" in Mission Trends No. 1, ed. by Gerald H. Anderson, and Thomas F. Stransky, (Toronto: Paulist Press, 1974) 243.

14. Raimundo Panikkar, "The Rules of the Game" in Mission Trends No. 5, ed. by Gerald H. Anderson, and Thomas F. Stransky, (Toronto: Paulist Press, 1981) 121.

15. Garaudy & Lauer, 30.

16. Norris, 22.

17. Thomas Dean, Post-Theistic Thinking: The Marxist-Christian Dialogue in Radical Perspective (Philadelphia: Temple University Press, 1975) 7.

18. Donald E. MacInnis, "Implications of China's Revolution" in Mission Trends No. 1, ed. by Gerald H. Anderson, and Thomas F. Stransky, (Toronto: Paulist Press, 1974) 276.

19. Dean, 230.

20. Christopher Mwolpka, "Trinity and Community" in Mission Trends No. 3, ed. by Gerald H. Anderson, and Thomas F. Stransky, (Toronto: Paulist Press, 1976) 154.

21. Dussel, 49.

22. Tissa Balasuriya, "An Asians Reflections after Vietnam" in Mission Trends No. 3, ed. by Gerald H. Anderson, and Thomas F. Stransky, (Toronto: Paulist Press, 1976) 249.

23. Montgomery, pp.129-30.

24. Samartha, 253.

25. Garaudy & Lauer, first quote p.74, second quote p.182.

26. Having lived and worked in the People's Republic of China from 1987 to 1988 I seem to agree with this view.

27. Nash, Ronald H. Poverty and Wealth. Westchester, Illinois: Crossway, 1986.

28. Dean, 8-9.

29. Dean, 39.

30. Dean, 35-36.

31.Gustavo Gorriti. "Peru's Prophet of Terror." Reader's Digest. Pleasantville, N.Y., September, 1992.

32. "Lima braces for rebel revenge attacks." Associated Press, The Orlando Sentinel, Tuesday, September, 15, 1992, A-3. Abimael Guzman is presently being held in jail awaiting either a life sentence in jail or execution.

33. Humberto Belli, 1985. Breaking Faith. Westchester, Illinois: Crossway Books, p.ix.

34. China is influenced by Daoist, Confusion, and Buddhist religious belief more than Christianity, thus the ideas they have implemented since the revolution probably reflect these religions more than Christianity.

35. Noel Leo Erskine, Decolonizing Theology: A Caribbean Perspective (Maryknoll, New York: Orbis Books, 1981) 119.

36. John Warwick Montgomery, "The Marxist Approach to Human Rights" in The Simon Greenleaf Law Review. Vol.III, 1983-84. p.21. Original sources: F. Engels, Feuerbach, The Roots of the Socialist Philosophy 58, 53. The second quote came from Feuerbach in Catlin's, The Story of the Political Philosophers 563.

37. The Holy Bible: New International Version of The New Testament and Psalms. (Grand Rapids, Michigan: Zondervan Bible Publishers, 1978) 322. I Corinthians 15:3-6, 12-15a, 17, 19.

38. Montgomery, p.124.

39. Gary R. Habermas, The Resurrection of Jesus. (Lanham, MD: University Press of America, 1984) 15.

40. Habermas, p.26.

41. Habermas, p.27.

42. McGovern, p.247.

43. Habermas, p.26.

44. McGovern, p.246.

45. J. P. Moreland. Scaling the Secular City: A Defense of Christianity. (Grand Rapids, Michigan: Baker Book House, 1987) 84.

46. Moreland, ch.3.

47. Montgomery, p.125-26.

48. Dean, 4-5.

49. Dussel, 165.

50. McGovern, 191.

51. Abraham Friesen, Reformation and Utopia: The Marxist Interpretation of the Reformation and its Antecedents (Wiesbaden: Franz Steiner Verlag Bmbh, 1974).

52. Walter Rauschenbusch, A Theology For The Social Gospel (New York: The MacMillan Company, 1918) 168.

53. Rauschenbusch, 184.

54. The Open Bible (New York: Thomas Nelson, Publishers, 1977) 188-189. This refers to Deut.26:5-9.

55. The Open Bible, Lev.18:24-28, p.111.

56. The Open Bible, Rom.3:26b, p.1084.

57. The Open Bible, Deut.15:7-8, p.180.

58. Montgomery, p.180. Original - Simon Greenleaf, The Testimony of the Evangelists.

Chapter Three, Continental/European Philosophy - Notes

1. Robert C. Walton, "Jurgen Moltmann's Theology of Hope - European Roots of Liberation Theology," in Liberation Theology. Edited by Ronald H. Nash, Grand Rapids, Michigan: Baker Book House, 1984, pp.139-186. Walton traces the specific European influences on liberation theology in this chapter.
2. Jerrold Katz, Semantic Theory (New York: Harper & Row, Publishers, 1972) 1.
3. Mildred L. Larson, Meaning-based Translation: A Guide to Cross-Language Equivalence (New York: University Press of America, 1984) 26.
4. John Beekman, John Callow, & Michael Kopesec, The Semantic Structure of Written Communication (Dallas, Texas: Summer Institute of Linguistics, 1981). Semantic structural analysis is the text preparation method of Wycliffe Bible Translators. It is a "proven" tool in providing a base text that can be translated into other languages with a very high degree of "message" content accuracy.
5. Harry P. Reeder, The Theory and Practice of Husserl's Phenomenology (New York: University Press of America, 1986) v.
6. Philip Pettit, On the Idea of Phenomenology (Dublin: Scepter Books, 1969) 10.
7. Stanely Deetz, Phenomenology In Rhetoric and Communication (Washington, D.C.: Center for Advanced Research in Phenomenology & University Press of America, 1981) 1.
8. Reeder, 1.
9. Edmund Husserl, Ideas: General Introduction to Pure Phenomenology (London: Collier Macmillan Publishers, 1931) 99-100.
10. Richard Lanigan, "The phenomenology of human communication." In Philosophy Today, Spring, 1977:7-8.
11. No mention will be made about the specifics of how the phoneme was found, outside of the bracketing of the traditional method. Any beginning linguistic text book will have an adequate account of "phoneme" specifics.
12. Josef Bleicher, Contemporary Hermeneutics: Hermeneutics as Method, Philosophy, and Critique (London: Routledge & Kegan Paul, 1980) 11.
13. Zygmunt Bauman, Hermeneutics and Social Science (New York: Columbia University Press, 1978) 148.
14. Bauman, 148-149.
15. Bleicher, 1-4.
16. Bleicher, 3-4.
17. Umberto Eco, A Theory of Semiotics (Bloomington: Indiana University Press, 1976) 7.
18. Kaja Silverman, The Subject of Semiotics (New York: Oxford University Press, 1983) 3.
19. Many of these terms and their definitions came from Dr. David N. Descutner's classical rhetoric course in the Winter of 1986 at Ohio University, Athens, Ohio.
20. Michael Lane, Introduction to Structuralism (New York: Basic Books, 1970) 18.
21. Terence Hawkes, Structuralism and Semiotics, (Los Angeles, Calif: University of California Press, 1977) 11-15.

22. Jean Piaget, Structuralism (New York: Basic Books, 1970) 5.
23. Hawks, 15-17.
24. Hawks, 18.
25. John Fekete (ed.), The Structural Allegory: Reconstruction Encounters with the New French Thought (Minneapolis: University of Minnesota Press, 1984) xv.
26. David Lodge, Working with Structuralism (Boston: Routledge & Kegan Paul, 1981) ix.

Chapter Five, Analysis - Notes

1. Arthur F. McGovern, Marxism: An American Christian Perspective (Maryknoll, New York: Orbis Books, 1984) 177.
2. Gustavo Gutierrez, A Theology of Liberation (Maryknoll, New York: Orbis Books, 1973). Gutierrez has republished "A Theology of Liberation" in 1988. His propositions remained nearly the same, thus for nearly twenty years his thinking has not changed significantly.
   Dennis P. McCann, "The Developing Gutierrez." Commonwealth. Vol.115, Issue 19, Number 4, Nov.4,1988. pp.594-595. Two distinct differences in Gutierrez' updated version include:
   ...sexist abstractions like "man" must now be rendered in such appropriately inclusive terms as "humanity." p.594.
   "Christian Fellowship and Class Struggle" has been substantially rewritten as "Faith and Social Conflict" ... the change is in the direction of inclusiveness, but ironically one that opens up a critical distance between liberation theology and Marxism. p.594.
3. Edward Cleary, a Dominican Priest who spoke on liberation theology at Ohio University, Athens, Ohio, on May 12, 1987, indicated that Gutierrez's writing style indeed represented a spider-web style rather than a logical format of a Western approach. Thus, it is a bit difficult to give a completely accurate outline format of his work.
4. This point could be challenged by anthropologists who say that "every" society tries to encompass reality with a world-view that answers all the basic questions such as the meaning of life, life after death, etc., thus, complete theology building "is" natural. Also, Gutierrez may not be aware of any "skewing," so we must be on our guard more because of the ability of symbolic phenomena to trick us with logically sounding arguments based on skewed premises, rather than on guarding against possible manipulation strategies of the author.
5. Dieter T. Hessel, "Introduction: A Liberating Approach To The Lectionary," Social Themes of the Christian Year, ed. Dieter T. Hessel (Philadelphia: The Geneva Press, 1983) 27.
6. Leonardo Boff, Church: Charism and Power (New York: Crossroad, 1985) 47.
   Joseph Comblin, "What Sort of Service Might Theology Render?" Frontiers of Theology in Latin America (Maryknoll, New York: Orbis Books, 1979). Comblin makes the same assertion as the following quote indicates:
   "The real question at stake for theology is whether people do or do not possess the language of God and its use. It must see to it that God's language ceases to be the private property of certain privileged classes, that the common people rise out of their shameful state once again."p.64.

7. Luis G. del Valle, "A Theological Outlook Starting from Concrete Events," Frontiers of Theology in Latin America, ed. Rosino Gibellini (Maryknoll, New York: Orbis Books, 1979) 86.

8. Valle, 93.

9. Sergio Torres, "Introduction" eds. Sergio Torres, and Virginia Fabella, M. M. The Emergent Gospel (Maryknoll, New York: Orbis Books, 1978) vii.

10. Gustavo Gutierrez, "Speaking about God" eds. Claude Greffre, Gustavo Gutierrez, and Virgil Elizondo, "Different Theologies, Common Responsibility: Babel or Pentecost?" Concilium 171 (Edinburgh: T. & T. Clark LTD, 1984) 28.

11. Gutierrez, 1984, p.29.

12. Gutierrez, 1984, p.31.

13. Philip Hefner, "Theology Engagee: Liberational, Political, Critical" Dialog vol.13, 1974:190.

14. Frederick Herzog, "Liberation Hermeneutic as Ideology Critique?" Interpretation vol. 28, no. 4, Oct. 1974:401.

15. Gustavo Gutierrez, "Liberation Praxis and Christian Faith," ed. Rosino Gibellini, Frontiers of Theology in Latin America (Maryknoll, New York: Orbis Books, 1979) 19.

16. Leonardo Boff, Church: Charism and Power (New York: Crossroad, 1985) 1.

17. Harold O. J. Brown, "True and False Liberation in the Light of Scripture," eds. Kenneth S. Kantzer, and Stanley N. Gundry, Perspectives on Evangelical Theology (Grand Rapids, Michigan: Baker Book House, 1979) 143.

18. Robert C. Walton, "Jurgen Moltmann's Theology of Hope." in Liberation Theology, edited by Ronald H. Nash. Baker Book House, 1984, pp.139-186. In this article Walton traces the specific European influences upon liberation thinkers like Gutierrez, and raises serious questions to Gutierrez' notion of how Christians are to be in the world.

19. Dow Kirkpatrick, "Liberation Theologians and Third World Demands" Christian Century vol.93, 1976:458.

20. Nash, Ronald & Humberto Belli, Beyond Liberation Theology. (Grand Rapids, Michigan: Baker Book House, 1992) 136-137. Nash refers to the "practice of blaming others and failing to look critically at themselves" as a Latin American cultural tendency, thus blaming everything on "developmentalism" is just another manifestation of this tendency. Nash ultimately suggests that harder and smarter work within a free democratic capitalistic system would materially liberate quicker than anything.

21. Kirkpatrick, 459.

22. Rene De Visme Williamson, "The Theology of Liberation," Christianity Today, 8 Aug. 1975:12.

23. Umberto Eco, "A Portrait of the Elder as a Young Pliny: How to Build Fame," ed. Marshall Blonsky, On Signs (Baltimore, Maryland: The John Hopkins University Press, 1985) 289-302.

24. McGovern, 13.

25. Starr Bowen, "Land Invasion and the Gospel" The Christian Century vol. 102, 11-18 Sept. 1985:800.

26. Bowen, 800.

27. A Chicago Reflection Group, "Exploring the Meaning of Liberation," eds. Sergin Torres, and John Eagleson, Theology in the Americas (Maryknoll, New York: Orbis Books, 1976) 217.

28. McGovern, 210-236.

29. Frederick Herzog, "Liberation Theology Begins at Home," Christianity and Crisis, 13 May. 1974:94-98.
30. Gregory Baum, "Faith And Liberation: Development Since Vatican II," ed. Gerald M. Fagin, Vatican II (Wilmington, Delaware: Michael Glazier, Inc., 1984) 98.
31. Baum, 98.
32. Baum, 99.
33. Baum, 99.
34. Baum, 100.
35. Helmut Gollwitzer, "Liberation in History" Interpretation vol. 28, no.4, Oct. 1974:420. Quoted in Roger Garaudy, From Anathema to Dialogue: The Challenge of Marxist Christian Cooperation, trans. by Luke O'Neill (New York: Herder and Herder, 1966) 98.
36. Good News Bible (New York: American Bible Society, 1976) 215-216.
37. Carolyn Cook Dipboye, "The Roman Catholic Church and the Political Struggle for Human Rights in Latin America, 1968-1980," Journal of Church and State, vol. 24, no. 3, 1982:495-524.
38. Dipboye, 500.
39. Dipboye, 500.
40. Dipboye, 506.
41. Dipboye, 510.
42. Thomas Niehaus, and Brady Tyson, "The Catholic Right in Contemporary Brazil: The Case of the Society for the Defense of Tradition, Family, and Property (TFP)" ed. Lyle C. Brown, Religion in Latin American Life and Literature (Waco, Texas: Markham Press Fund, 1980) 394-409.
43. E. Bradford Burns, Latin America (Englewood Cliffs, New Jersey: Prentice-Hall, Inc. 1986) 339.
44. Penny Lernoux, Cry of the People (New York: Penguin Books, 1980) 83. Lernoux used the following information for documentation of this incident: "The Republic of Nicaragua: An Amnesty International Report Including the Findings of a Mission to Nicaragua, May 10-15, 1976 (London), p.27; also author's interviews in Zelaya (Mar. 1977), and letters to author from U.S. Capuchins in Nicaragua (May 20, June 13, and Oct. 16, 1977)." This information can be found on p.483 of Lernoux's book.
45. Lernoux, 203. This quote came from Nathaniel Davis, U.S. ambassador to Guatemala, addressing the U.S. Chamber of Commerce meeting in Guatemala, April 20, 1971, found in "United Fruit Is Not Chiquita" (North American Congress on Latin America, Oct. 1971), p.7.
46. Robert McAffee Brown, "Drinking from Our Own Wells" The Christian Century vol.101, 1984:485.
47. Brown, 486.
48. Gutierrez, 1979, p.17.
49. Gutierrez, 1973, p.275.
50. Michael Novak, "Liberation Theology and The Pope" ed. Quentin L. Quade, The Pope and Revolution (Washington, D.C.: Ethics and Public Policy Center, 1982) 84.
51. Gustavo Gutierrez, "Liberation Theology and Progressivist Theology" eds. Sergio Torres, and Virginia Fabella, M. M. The Emergent Gospel (Maryknoll, New York: Orbis Books, 1978) 228.
52. Gutierrez, 1978, p.231.

53. Gutierrez, 1978, p.235.

54. Gutierrez, 1978. p.240.

55. "Statement by Enrique Dussel," eds. Sergin Torres, and John Eagleson, Theology in the Americas (Maryknoll, New York: Orbis Books, 1976) 287.

56. A Chicago Reflection Group, 239.

57. Paul Morgan and Edd Noell. 1990. "Capitalism and Liberation Theology in Latin America." Unpublished paper. Westmont College, Dept. of Business & Economics, 955 La Paz Road, Santa Barbara, 93108-1099.

58. Ibid, 8-9.

59. Richard N. Ostling, "A Lesson On Liberation" Time vol. 127, 14 Ap. 1986:84.

60. George Russell, "Taming the Liberation Theologians" Time vol. 125, 4 Feb. 1985:56.

61. "Revolutionary Antagonism and Christian Love" Church and Society vol.65, 1975:25.

62. L. Michael Jendrzejczyk, "Peace and Liberation Groups Confer," Christian Century 9 May. 1984:480.

63. Jose Miguez Bonino, "Violence & Liberation," Christianity and Crisis, 10 July. 1972:171.

64. Bonino, 171.

65. Bonino, 172.

66. Paul G. King, and David D. Woodyard, The Journey Toward Freedom: Economic Structures and Theological Perspectives (London: Associated University Press, 1982) 146.

67. Gutierrez, 11.

68. Gutierrez, 1979, p.11.

69. "A New Attitude" Christianity Today 5 Sept. 1986:48.

70. Dean C. Curry, A World Without Tyranny. (Westchester, Illinois: Crossway Books, 1990) 245-246.

71. Rev. Donald J. Keefe, S.J., "Liberation and the Catholic Church: The Illusion and the Reality," Center Journal vol.1, 1981:57.

72. King & Woodyard, 14.

73. King & Woodyard, 14.

74. John A. Coleman, "Civil Religion and Liberation Theology," ed. Sergin Torres, and John Eagleson, Theology in the Americas (Maryknoll, New York: Orbis Books, 1976) 131.

75. "Statement by Gustavo Gutierrez," ed. Sergin Torres, and John Eagleson, Theology in the Americas (Maryknoll, New York: Orbis Books, 1976) 311.

76. Michael Dodson, "The Christian Left in Latin American Politics," ed. Daniel H. Levine, Churches and Politics in Latin America (London: Sage Publications, 1979) 118.

77. Margaret Crahan, "Salvation Through Christ or Marx," ed. Daniel H. Levine, Churches and Politics in Latin America (London: Sage Publications, 1979) 263.

78. Good New Bible, 269.

79. Boff, 1985, p.125.

80. Boff, 1985, pp.125-130.

81. Lernoux, 85.

82. Lernoux, 85.

83. Boff, 1985, p.132.

84. Boff, 1985, pp.154-164.

85. Darrell Holland, "Bishops Propose Guaranteed Jobs For Poor" The Plain Dealer 14 Nov. 1986:2-Aw.

86. Burns, 349.

87. James R. Brockman, S.J., "The Prophetic Role of the Church in Latin America" The Christian Century vol.100, 1983:932.

88. James H. Cone, "Black Theology and the Black Church," eds. Gerald H. Anderson, and Thomas F. Stransky, Mission Trends No. 4 (Grand Rapids, Michigan: Wm. B. Eerdmans Publishing Co., 1979) 142.

89. Elizabeth Schussler Fiorenza, "Feminist Theology as a Critical Theology of Liberation," eds. Gerald H. Anderson, and Thomas F. Stransky, Mission Trends No. 4 (Grand Rapids, Michigan: Wm. B. Eerdmans Publishing Co., 1979) 190.

90. Quade, 58.

91. Clark H. Pinnock, "Liberation Theology: The Gains, The Gaps," Christianity Today, 16 Jan. 1976:14.

92. R. T. France, "Liberation in the New Testament," The Evangelical Quarterly, vol. 58, no.1, 1986:21.

93. Quade, 52.

94. Arthur G. Gish, The New Left and Christian Radicalism (Grand Rapids, Michigan: Wm. B. Eerdmans Publishing Co., 1970) 75.

95. Raymond K. Dehainaut, Faith and Ideology in Latin-American Perspective (Cuernavaca, Mexico: Comite Directivo De Publicaciones, 1972) 6/39-6/41.

96. Dehainaut, 6/41.

97. The Open Bible, Amos 2:6-7, p.837. Gutierrez uses this passage in A Theology of Liberation, on p.293.

98. Beatriz Melano Couch, "New Vision of the Church in Latin America" eds. Sergio Torres, and Virginia Fabella, M. M. The Emergent Gospel (Maryknoll, New York: Orbis Books, 1978) 220.

99. "To Walk With the Church" America 152, 6 Ap. 1985:265.

100. "To Walk With the Church," 265.

101. "Boff Silenced" Time 125, 20 May, 1985:44.

102. Associated Press, "Liberation theology founder quits Catholic Church." The Orlando Sentinel, Saturday, July 4, 1992, page C-7. The article went on to say that Boff released a new book entitled: "Latin America: From Conquest to the New Evangelization" which "shows how Christianity 'was used to legitimize oppression and injustice in Latin America' and calls on the church to become more sensitive to the plight of the poor."

103. Christine E. Gudorf, "Ratzinger, Gutierrez, & the bishops of Peru" Commonwealth vol. 112, 8 Feb. 1985:77.

104. Gudorf, 78.

105. Gustavo Gutierrez, "Liberation, Theology, and Proclamation" The Pope and Revolution (Washington, D.C.: Ethics and Public Policy Center, 1982) 33.

106. Williamson, 12-13.

107. W. Dayton Roberts, "Liberation Theologies: Looking at Poverty from the Under Side," Christianity Today, 17 May. 1985:15.

108. Roberts, 16.

109. Leslie R. Keylock, "The Vatican Tries to Rein In a Leading Proponent of Liberation Theology," Christianity Today 19 Oct. 1984:47.

110. Walter W. Benjamin, "Liberation Theology: European Hopelessness Exposes the Latin Hoax," Christianity Today 5 Mar. 1982:21.

111. Charles R. Strain, "Ideology and Alienation: Theses on the Interpretation and Evaluation of Theologies of Liberation," Journal of the American Academy of Religion, vol. 45, no. 4, 1977:473.

112. Thomas G. Sanders, "The Theology of Liberation: Christian Utopianism," Christianity and Crisis, 17 Sept. 1973:170.

Chapter Five, Conclusion - Notes

1. This proposition was given by Dr. Algis Mickunas, professor of philosophy, Ohio University, Athens, Ohio.

2. This proposition was given by Dr. Algis Mickunas of Ohio University, Athens, Ohio.

3. I do believe in progress, and that the basics of life are being increasingly provided for the poor. But I do not believe that humanity has learned to live in harmony or communally by building on a historical consciousness.

4. David Allan Hubbard, What We Evangelicals Believe. (Pasadena, California: Fuller Theological Seminary, 1979). In this book Hubbard briefly outlines the evangelical faith we share as follows:

- the eternal trinity;
- the reality of God's revelation in creation, history, and scripture;
- the creation of humankind in God's image and the subsequent fall through disobedience;
- the coming to earth in human flesh of God's eternal Son - born of a virgin, fully obedient to God, working miracles as signs of God's kingdom, crucified to bear our judgment and to reveal God's love, risen bodily from the dead, ascended to the Father's side;
- the work of the Holy Spirit who enables us to believe in Christ and grow in his grace
- the formation of the church to demonstrate God's love and to carry out God's mission in worship, nurture, evangelism and justice;
- the consummation of God's kingdom in the personal return of Jesus Christ which results in the resurrection of the race, the final separation of unbelievers from God's presence and the glorification of believers as they enjoy eternal fellowship with the triune God.

5. Ronald J. Sider, "An Evangelical Theology of Liberation," Christian Century 19 Mar. 1980:314-318.

6. Schubert M. Odgen, "The Concept of a Theology of Liberation: Must a Christian Theology Today Be So Conceived?" eds. Brian Mahan, and L. Dale Richesin, The Challenge of Liberation Theology: A First World Response (Maryknoll, New York: Orbis Books, 1981) 127-139.

7. Roy I. Sano, "Liberation: From What, For What?" ed. Dieter T. Hessel, Social Themes of the Christian Year (Philadelphia: The Geneva Press, 1983) 190-194.

8. Of course totalitarianism is very different from democracy, yet I'm convinced that the PROC would not practice socialism if they could vote on it! Socialism seems to require totalitarianism to exist.

9.Clark Pinnock, "A Pilgrimage In Political Theology" in Liberation Theology, edited by Ronald H. Nash, (Grand Rapids, Michigan: Baker Book House, 1984) 101-120. Here Pinnock wrote about his personal pilgrimage into the radical left. Even though Pinnock's experience was far more radical than mine, we both were swayed into thinking negatively about U.S. capitalism and the global benefits of democratic socialism. My wife and I returned from the PROC patriots of the basic system of democratic capitalism, and the necessity of political and religious freedom, yet pessimists about democratic socialism. It seems that taking away incentive kills motivation for working hard and smart within socialistic economic systems. Also, I agree with Ron Nash that democratic capitalism operating in a free society is morally and ethically superior to democratic socialism, and is more in tune with the divine creative nature of the human race. Plus, it has a concrete history for being able to liberate more than any other economic and political system to date.

10. An excellent overview of the strands of "millennialism" held in Christianity is The Last Days Handbook by Robert P. Lightner published by Nelson. Dr. Lightner is Professor of Systematic Theology at Dallas Theological Seminary.

11. Ronald H. Nash, "Toward a New Liberation Theology." Jackson, Mississippi: Encourager - Reformed Theological Seminary Alumni Newsletter, Spring, 1992, 9. This excerpt was taken out of Beyond Liberation Theology by Humberto Belli & Ronald H. Nash, published by Baker Book House, 1992.

INDEX

accept-respect vs.
  believe, 24
alienation, 25-30
Allende, Salvador, 69
Anabaptists, 97
Aquinas, Thomas, 56
base Christian comm.,
  5
Boff, Leonardo, 9, 58,
  100
Bonino, Jose Miguez,
  86
bracketing, 44
Brown, Robert
  McAffee, 81
center, 60
Centesimus Annus, 10
charisms, 89
charity, 56
class struggle, 81
Couch, Beatriz
Melano, 99
conscientization, 5
coercive violence, 76
critical reflection, 5
critical school, 7
democratic socialism,
  86
developmentalism, 66
dialectic, 1
dialogue foundations,
  20
divine inspiration, 2
eidetic, 45
empathy, 22
Enlai, Chou, 111
Eucharist, 98
European mercantilism,
  85
evangelical left, 12
feedback, 22
Fiorenza, Elizabeth S.,
  96
Frankfurt School, 15
Freire, Paulo, 6
gender prejudice, 5
Gutierrez, Gustavo, 3
Habermas, Gary, 32

Habermas, Jurgen, 14
Heidegger, Martin, 49
hermeneutics, 48
  classical, 49
  critical, 50
Hermes, 48
Herzog, Frederick, 62
humanization, 24-25
Husseral, Edmund, 43
institutional violence, 7
Jendrzejczyk, L. M.,
  85
Jesus' resurrection, 33
Keefe, Donald J., 87
killing vs. murder, 28
liberation theology, 1
Mao, Chairman, 111
markett economy, 11
martyrs, 92
Marx, Karl, 19
materialism, 20, 32
meaning, 42
Medellin Conference, 7
metatextuality, 45
mind/body dualism, 34
modern age, 83
mythical structures, 53
natural attitude, 15, 21
new hermeneutic, 1
Nash, Ronald H.,
  29, 101
Novak, Michael, 82
ontology, 49
oppression, 2
Orbis Books, 92
periphery, 60
phenomenology, 43
phoneme, 45
Piaget, Jean, 53
Pope Paul II, 10
post-millennial
  eschatology, 114
poverty, 4
praxis, 7, 20
race prejudice, 5
Ratzinger, Joseph, 99
Rauschenbusch,
Walter, 32

reified, 43
Roberts, W. Dayton,
  101
Romero, Oscar, 20
Sapir/Whorph
  hypothesis, 21
Sanders, Thomas G.,
  102
secularization, 67
self-disclosure, 22
semantics, 42
semiotics, 51
Sider, Ron, 111
social gospel, 1-2
socialism, 4
structuralism, 52
tension, 60
texts, 10
tools, 41
Torres, Sergio, 60
traditional theology, 1
trust, 22
Valle, Luis G. del, 59
Vico, Giambattist, 53
violence, 30

About the Author

Dr. J. David Turner is a pastor, professor, and author. He has a B.A. in Theology, an M.A. in Linguistics, and a Ph.D. in Rhetoric and Public Address. In 1988 he was a foreign expert teaching in Chongqing, People's Republic of China; Director of the English as a Second Language Department at the University of Nevada, Las Vegas in 1990; Visiting Assistant Professor at Westmont College in Santa Barbara, California in 1991; and Assistant Pastor of Sonlife Community Church in Lake Mary, Florida in 1992. Currently Dr. Turner is an Adjunct Professor at Warner Southern College in Orlando, Florida where He and his wife Jan live with their daughter Faye Marie.